Examining the Record

Martin Luther King, Jr. Memorial Studies in Religion, Culture and Social Development

Mozella G. Mitchell
General Editor

Vol. 4

PETER LANG
New York • Washington, D.C./Baltimore • San Francisco
Bern • Frankfurt am Main • Berlin • Vienna • Paris

Alvin A. Jackson

Examining the Record

An Exegetical and Homiletical Study of Blacks in the Bible

PETER LANG
New York • Washington, D.C./Baltimore • San Francisco
Bern • Frankfurt am Main • Berlin • Vienna • Paris

Library of Congress Cataloging-in-Publication Data

Jackson, Alvin Andre.
   Examining the record: an exegetical and homiletical study of Blacks in
the Bible / Alvin Andre Jackson.
      p.   cm. — (Martin Luther King, Jr. memorial studies in religion,
culture, and social development; vol. 4)
   Includes bibliographical references.
   1. Blacks in the Bible.   2. Bible—Biography.   I. Title.   II. Series.
   BS680.B48J34   1994   220.'305896—dc20   93-42799
   ISBN 0-8204-2389-0   CIP
   ISSN 1052-181X

Die Deutsche Bibliothek-CIP-Einheitsaufnahme

Jackson, Alvin A.:
Examining the record: an exegetical and homiletical study of Blacks in the
Bible / Alvin A. Jackson. - New York; Washington D.C./Baltimore;
San Francisco; Bern; Frankfurt am Main; Berlin; Vienna; Paris: Lang, 1994
   (Martin Luther King, Jr. memorial studies in religion, culture, and social
   development; Vol. 4)
   ISBN 0-8204-2389-0
NE: GT

Photo on back cover by Tom Halliwell.

Cover design by Geraldine Spellissy.

The paper in this book meets the guidelines for permanence and durability of
the Committee on Production Guidelines for Book Longevity of the
Council on Library Resources.

Printed in the United States of America.

TABLE OF CONTENTS

ACKNOWLEDGEMENTS

I am profoundly indebted to God for the endless stream of material that He has directed to me from a multitude of sources that has fed me mentally, spiritually, and emotionally. I am deeply indebted to my mentor and faculty friend, Dr. Thomas McDaniel whose gentle but persistent nudging and input—the result of many years of analysis, searching and investigation —has encouraged me to initiate this work. I am deeply indebted to my dear wife, Ann, whose acquired typing skills have enhanced her ability to use our computer to make endless drafts of this project and for her indefatigable zeal that encouraged me to persevere. I am also deeply indebted to the Saint Paul Baptist Church family of Cinnaminson, New Jersey, for their encouragement and prayers and to the many friends, too numerable to list, whose words became refreshing incentives that echoed in my memory when I grew weary. Moreover, to the Blockson Collections of Temple University for the wealth of material made accessible to me, I am very grateful.

Examining the Record

PART ONE: EXEGETICAL STUDIES

INTRODUCTION

Alex Beam wrote a brief article in the August 22, 1991 *Philadelphia Inquirer* which began with the headline "Africa may hold truth about Western roots." In it he addressed the debate created by the publication of Martin Bernal's massive two volume study entitled *Black Athena*[1] which attempts to move critical scholarship in Classical and Near Eastern Studies from a Eurocentric to an Afrocentric base. Beam noted, "Ironically, even archaeologists who can prove that Bernal's methodology is flawed agree with his central premise — that Egypt and the Levant profoundly influenced ancient Greece."

Len Cooper followed Alex Beam with a similar article in *The Washington Post* of September 14, 1991, under the headline "Bible scholars aim to show African influence in a new light." In this article, Cooper addressed the current efforts to reverse the traditional "de-Africanization" of the Bible. He cited Cain Hope Felder, who stated:

> We have before us the opportunity of a new cultural renaissance through theological interpretation of biblical scholarship . . . . To make the Bible totally black as the Black Yahwist[2] has done would be as bad as what [white scholars] have done by taking us out of the Bible and marginalizing us.

Cooper also cited Ephraim Isaac, an Ethiopian Jew who is professor at the Institute of Semitic Languages at Princeton, who noted:

> I find that African American leadership in this country forcefully supports European history [when isolating Egypt and Ethiopia from Africa]. Biblically, ancient Greece connects Africa to Europe, but its the Ethiopian Church (the oldest Christian Church in Africa that connects American Christians to Africa.)

On September 23, 1991, *Newsweek* carried on its front cover the question, "Was Cleopatra Black?" Inside was an eight page article which covered the current debate over Martin Bernal's *Black Athena*.[3]

This thesis essay can be seen as my contribution to the current discussion on the re-Africanization of some of the biblical traditions. As will be obvious, this essay will not participate in the debate over Martin Bernal's *Black Athena*, for this debate will have to be carried on by the specialized academicians. But it will attempt to present a resource for preaching from those biblical texts and related traditions which deal with Blacks in the Bible.

There are several works available dealing with Blacks in the Bible, but they are weak on the exegetical component essential for effective preaching. Perhaps the best known of these earlier books is Dunstan's 1974 study, *The Black Man in the Old Testament and its World*. But as Adamo (1986: 9) indicated, with reference to its value for writing his dissertation,

> However without denying that his book will be useful in this dissertation, his work is inadequate. It is mostly based on the English Version (King James Version). . . The chapters on Egypt and Cush (or Kush) were dealt with in "a cursory manner."

Adamo's Ph.D. dissertation (Baylor University), which became available to me only at the conclusion of my work on this thesis essay, is an excellent study. As a specialist in biblical studies, with control of the biblical languages, Adamo provides good exegesis and good summaries in the history of interpretation of the various biblical texts. But his focus is not on application to preaching on the texts he explores.

I have avoided the approach taken by Walter McCray in his two volume study, *The Black Presence in the Bible*. He stated, for example,

> Through Biblical word studies it is easily demonstrable that Black peoples are present in the Scripture by virtue of their names which bespeak their identity (e.g. "Cush" or "Kedar"). On the basis of physical anthropological, archaeological, historical, cultural studies and the like, it can be demonstrated that Biblical peoples are "Black." (Volume 2: 3)

I have followed Cain Hope Felder, in this regard, who recognized that making the Biblical world all black was no more credible than making it all white.

Since early childhood, I have been very curious about the absence of Black persons of note in the Biblical history as it was presented to me. It seemed that there was an overwhelming preponderance of white individuals that tenaciously usurp the entire stage of historical and interpersonal interactions in the drama of life. Subsequently, I had the question arise, "Is this sacred history a record to exalt and magnify the importance of only those of the caucasian race?" I was cognizant that this is a sacred record of God's omnipotence involved in the life of a chosen few, namely, those of the Hebrew nation. But as a Black, I came to ask myself, "Are we Blacks being brainwashed either by the mental superiority or the spiritual excellence or the peculiar divine selection of the transcendent engineer of all things in all life?" or "Is this the unquestioned design of the awesome yet magnificent creator of the universe?"

If this is so, a host of other questions follow: what are we to understand regarding the words, "God is no respecter of persons"? Are the singular qualities that make a person bold, sincere, fearless, God-conscious, or supernaturally imbued, only for the white race? Are we in possession of the whole truth of the present scriptures or have some details of revealing significance purposely deleted? Have the scriptures been correctly understood?

I recognized early that no ethnic division in the human family is present in the text until the "confusion of tongues" at the tower of Babel. No racial reference can be found in Genesis. The nearest we can come to the evidence of Black skin color in the scriptures is in the words Cush (Kush), Ham, or terms that are derived from the family of Ham.

Are these the only references of importance about the presence of Blacks in the scriptures? Unable to suppress the mounting desire to find the answer to these long standing questions and related issues, I initiated my investigation and commenced this component of my Doctor of Ministry program. To my delight, I found that there were many scholars and writers who had been aroused by the same unanswered queries, the most recent of whom I have noted above.

In this study I will provide an exegetical study of major biblical figures who were a part of the Black presence in the Bible. This part of the thesis essay will be followed by a series of sermons preached in my church, the Saint Paul Baptist Church of Cinnaminson, New

Jersey, in 1991 – 1992, using as the sermon texts those passages which were exegeted as a part of the research component.

THE CURSE OF HAM AND ITS IMPLICATION

It is no secret that Genesis 9:18–29 was commonly used to legitimate slavery in the Americas and elsewhere. As the historian William McKee Evans (1980: 26) noted,

> Probably as late as the seventh century A.D. more local natives than blacks were sold as slaves in the Near East. Before the establishment of Islam [the Near East] itself supplied considerable numbers of captives to the slave trade. It may have been as late as A.D. 1000 before the institution of slavery in the Near East and Muslim lands became predominantly Negro slavery. . . . But long before a majority of slaves were black, perhaps several centuries before, enough Africans were sold *in the Near East* [italics mine] to form the basis for a racial stereotype farther west. . . . This bottom stratum of society which included only a small minority of the white population . . . became the instantly visible "Canaanites," the archetypal "sons of Ham."

Felder (1989: 38), in his discussion of race and sacralization, noted,

> We shall consider the so-called curse of Ham (Gen. 9:18–27), which rabbis of the early Talmudic periods and the Church Fathers at times used to denigrate Black people. Later Europeans adopted the so-called curse of Ham as a justification for slavery and stereotypical aspersions about Blacks.[4]

Plaut (1974: 83) commenting on Gen 9:25, noted as a corrective, "Advocates of the black man's slavery used to base their beliefs on this text, but this passage deals with political subjection and has nothing whatsoever to do with race." Typical of those who, in more recent times, so used this text was Thornton Stringfellow of Culpeper County, Virginia, who in 1856 began his pamphlet entitled *Scriptural and Statistical Views in Favor of Slavery*[5] by proclaiming:

> The first recorded language which was ever uttered in relation to slavery, is the inspired language of Noah. In God's stead he says, "Cursed be Canaan;" "a servant of servants shall he be to his brethren." "Blessed be the Lord God of Shem; and Canaan shall be his servant." "God shall enlarge Japheth, and he shall dwell in the tents of Shem; and Canaan shall be his servant." — Gen. ix:25, 26, 27. Here, language is used, showing the *favor* which God would exercise to the posterity of Shem and Japheth, while they were holding the posterity of Ham in a state of

abject bondage. May it not be said in truth, that God decreed this institution before it existed; and has he not connected its *existence* with prophetic tokens of special favor, to those who should be slave owners and masters?

However, the past century has witnessed great change and it is not surprising to have Evans (1980: 15) reflect current (majority) opinion when he writes,

> This strange story [of the curse of Canaan] has troubled theologians for perhaps two thousand years. Since it is first found in the Old Testament, a common source of the Jewish, Christian, and Muslim traditions, moralists have understandably expected to find in it some illustration of ethics or justice. Yet the story offends our moral sensibilities at almost every point. In the first place, even with the extreme sensitivity that the ancient Hebrews are supposed to have had about nudity is taken into account, Noah's curse dwarfs Ham's offense. By any ordinary standard, ancient or modern, Noah overreacted. Second, the curse fell not upon the offender at all, but upon Canaan, a son of Ham, who, in terms of the story, is totally innocent.

Evans correctly noted that "as yet [in the first millennium B. C.] the tradition showed no color bias," for the Hebrews did not associate slavery with any particular race. It was racially nonspecific. His study of the shifting ethnic identifications of the "sons of Ham" (as a way of learning something about the historical pressures that shaped modern white racial attitudes) warrants careful reading.[6] However, the focus of our study here is on meaning and interpretation of the biblical text.

The text concerning the "curse of Ham" as found in Genesis 9:18–29 is full of exegetical problems, many of which have not been adequately explained. The following literalistic translation of Rosenberg (1990: 72–73) reflects the way in which a contemporary translator subjectively interprets the text to legitimate Noah's curse of Canaan by exaggerating the offense of Ham.

> So it was: Noah, who tills the soil, is the first to plant a vineyard. Now he drank from the wine, now he was drunk, now he lay uncovered in the middle of his tent. The one who fathered Canaan, Ham, *enjoyed* (italics mine) his father's nakedness: now he tells it to the two brothers outside. But Shem and Yafat took a cloak, draped it over their shoulders, walked in backward, covered their naked father, faces averted: they never saw their father naked. Roused from his wine, Noah learned what happened, what his youngest son made of him. "A bitter curse on Canaan," he said. "A servant to his brothers' servants. A blessing on Yahweh, Shem's God," he said. "But Canaan — his servant. God will fatten Yafat, make him welcome in Shem's tents. But Canaan — his servant."

Bloom's (1990: 189-190) recent interpretation, based upon Rosenberg's translation, but reflecting longstanding Jewish exegesis, is as follows:[7]

> We are back in the mode of what we call children's literature, if indeed we have ever left it. The Deluge over, the propitiated Yahweh smells "a soothing scent" (26) and is to declare that there will be no more mass destructions of people or of animals. This seems a fit Yahweh for Noah, the first alcoholic, so splendidly celebrated in a poem by G. K. Chesterton in which the most righteous of his generation chants refrain, "I don't care where the water goes if it doesn't get into the wine." I begin to feel redundant in my instance that [the author] J is a comic writer when we come to the story of Noah and his sons. I have some suspicions that J's exuberance has been censored here, and that Noah did not merely observe his father's pudendum. When Noah "lay uncovered in the middle of the tent," he presumably was enjoying his wife, "tent" being a plausible metaphor for the lady, and there is an uncomfortable edge in the statement that Ham "enjoyed his father's nakedness," almost as though sodomy is suggested. We certainly enjoy the hilariously respectful performance of Shem and Yafat. . . .

> These two ingenious young men receive their reward; Ham's son Canaan is cursed, while Shem and Yafat are allied in mastery over Canaan. Historians read this as alluding to an uneasy joint stance of the twelfth-century Hebrews and Philistines against the native Canaanites,[8] but I am inclined to read it as another instance of J's humor. So outrageous is the episode of Noah and his sons that the political allegory must have been just as deliberately rancid. Evidently, Canaan had a somewhat freer mode of sexuality than post-Solomonic Jerusalem overtly manifested, and perhaps J's Noah and the Flood story has little or no special significance for her, unlike P's solemn rendition, which is an account of the First Covenant. Incessant ironist though she was, J seems to have enjoyed Flood, ark, and Noah each for its own sake alone. (189-190)

Sarna (1989: 64-65) subtitled this section of Genesis "The Depravity of Canaan," and gave the following introductory comments:

> The section deals with Noah as a culture hero who introduced viticulture and who fell victim to his progeny's depravity. Because the original incidents, in all their detail, were well known to the biblical audience and for reasons of delicate sensibility, only the barest outline of his [Canaan's] downfall is reported here. The fuller account, now lost, has been truncated and condensed, resulting in the many difficulties we now find in the narrative. For instance, we are not certain if Ham is guilty solely of voyeurism or if the description of his offense in verse 22 is a euphemism for some act of gross indecency; we are not told why Noah curses Canaan and not Ham. (64-65)

The interpretations of Sarna and Rosenberg are sufficient to highlight the problems involved with this text. They are basically as follows:

(1)   What was the offense that prompted Noah to curse Canaan?
(2)   Why was Canaan cursed and not Ham?
(3)   What is meant by "uncovering the father's nakedness"?
(4)   What other possible act could be involved in the offense of Noah.

Speiser (1964: 61) believes that Ham literally saw his father naked. The specific reference, he believes, is to the pudenda, which refers to the external genitals of either sex. According to Speiser the term *'erwat* itself relates to exposure and does not of necessity imply any sexual offense. In contrast to Speiser, Bassett (1971: 232–239), like Bloom and Sarna, cited above, suggests that some of the tradition has been lost precluding the success of critical scholars in their attempt to reconstruct the original story. The Hebrew text of Genesis 9:22 states simply and clearly that Ham simply *saw* (contra Rosenberg's "enjoyed") Noah lying intoxicated and exposed in his tent: "Ham saw the pudenda of his father (*wayyar' 'et 'erwat 'ăbî*) and told (*wayygēd*) his brothers" who were outside (*bahûs*) the tent (contra Targum Neophyti's translation which had Ham publicly slandering his father: "And Ham, the father of the Canaanites saw the nakedness of his father and told his two brothers in the marketplace [*besûqâ*]").

We are thus led to believe by numerous commentators that Ham showed bold disrespect by observing the nakedness of his father and added to this the affront by telling what he had observed to his brothers in the public market. He had entered into his father's tent, but although there is no reference as to whether or not Noah's wife was also in the tent, exegetes have been pleased to introduce her to make the offense of Ham all the more repugnant, hence the curse was all the more deserved. In the text there is not the slightest hint that she may have been in the same tent with the inebriated and unconscious Noah. Nevertheless, with his father in this condition, some have conjectured, Ham could have violated his mother.[9]

As noted already, Ham's actions do not seem adequate an offense to provoke a curse from his father. It is, therefore, believed by some that something more volatile must have transpired. Ancient Jewish traditions cited by Ginzberg (1925 1: 168) suggests that Ham, for unknown reasons, castrated his father in an effort to prevent him from continued propagation. Other sources claim that Ham's son, Canaan, castrated Noah by looping a cord about his genitals and drawing it tight to close off the circulation of life-giving blood. Thus the "curse of Canaan." Ham's guilt in the latter instance would have been that he saw what Canaan did and expressed his approval by conveying the violent incident against his father to his brothers.

Ginzberg (1925 1: 169) suggests that Canaan, the grandson of Noah, had to suffer vicariously for the sin of his own father because God had already conferred blessings upon Noah and his three sons as they departed from the Ark, making Ham untouchable for a curse. Finding some valid justification for the horrendous curse is the reason for these far-fetched traditions. However, there is no basis in the biblical text for giving historical credibility to any of these traditions or translations.

Ginzberg (1925 5: 188) also notes another tradition that during the days Noah and his family stayed in the Ark along with the animals, the family and the animals, alike, were separated by sex because in case of a public calamity, such as the flood, sexual continence was to be practiced by all who have been spared. According to one tradition, this "law of social conduct" was violated in the Ark by Ham, by the dogs, and by the ravens. Each of these was, in turn, punished for the violation of this law. It is important to note that contrary to some interpretations of this tradition, there is no statement that Ham had sex with the dog and the raven, and was thus guilty of bestiality and all the more deserving of the curse of slavery.

The punishment according to *Midrash Tanhuma'* for the ravens was that they become "worthless, good for nothing." (McDaniel notes that the word is *raqa'*, which is the same word behind the Greek *raka* "fool" in Matt. 5:22; the raven did not have sense enough to return to the ark when it couldn't find dry land.) The dogs were punished by becoming "knotted" when having sexual intercourse. Ham, because (1) he saw his father's pudendum *with his eyes*, his eyes would be reddened, (2) because he told his brothers with his mouth, his lips would protrude, and (3) because he turned his face, the hair of his head and beard would be singed. According to *Yalqut Shem'oni* Ham would have moist skin (i.e., sweat and smell).

While these traditions reflect stereotyping, it is of interest that no reference is made to color, save for red eyes. Contrary to McCray (1990: 70) who states, "The name 'Ham' means 'hot,' 'heat,' and by application, 'black'," these Jewish traditions make no connection between Ham and blackness, no connection between the curse of Ham/Canaan and *skin* color. According to Ginzberg, the underlying idea of this legend was that "the individual should participate in the sufferings of the community."

With reference to the alleged sodomy of Ham, it needs to be noted that homosexual practices were not prohibited in the book of the covenant nor in the book of Deuteronomy, but were made criminal in the holiness code as found in Leviticus 18:22; and 20:13. These provisions according to Phillips (1980: 38–43) are to govern all sexual relationships between males, rather than specifically deal with the case of a son molesting his father. The idiomatic euphemism used in the law meaning to have sexual intercourse is *gilleh 'erwat* "to uncover the pudendum (of someone)." As spelled out in Lev 18: 6–19, a man is not to *uncover* the nakedness of (i.e., "to have sex with") his sister, nor of his father's daughter, nor of his mother's daughters, etc., for it was considered a criminal offense and those who were guilty of such offense were "to be cut off from their people" (Lev. 18: 29), i.e., "put to death" (Lev. 20:10), "they shall die childless" (Lev. 20: 20), the same as if they had sacrificed to the god Molech or profaned the name of God.[10]

To those who have wanted to equate "seeing the pudenda" with "uncovering the pudendum" (see Lev. 20: 17) it would seem that a later editor or redactor actually missed the idiomatic meaning in the tradition that "Ham saw (i.e., *uncovered*) his father's nakedness (i.e., *had sex with*) and added that part of the story which refers to the other two sons of Noah covering their fathers exposed body with a garment so as not to literally *see* him (nothing more, nothing other than *sight*).

The question arose very early, "How did Canaan get involved in the curse?" for he was, seemingly, not there at the time of the incident. However, as noted above, he was made by some to be the original offender. Skinner (1910: 184) believed that there were two different genealogical schemes: one (implicitly) recognized Noah's children as being Shem, Japheth, and Canaan (since in 9:26 Shem and Japheth are referred to as the *brothers* of Canaan); the other, explicitly, spoke of Shem, Ham, and Japheth).

Speiser (1964: 62) summarized the issues:

> the explicit order of the sons of Noah, which indicates age, is invariably Shem—Ham—Japheth; see v 32, vi 10, vii 13, ix 18, x 1. Accordingly one is not prepared for the notation in 24 that Ham was the youngest. At most he should have been called "the younger," but Hebrew cannot be forced to yield this meaning. Two possible explanations suggest themselves: (1) the passage before us derives from a different tradition, one in which either Ham or Canaan was cited as the third son of Noah; this is the view of most modern critics. (2) The statement refers not to Noah's youngest son, but Ham's . . . Ham himself, then would be the offended party and his son Canaan the perpetrator of some base deed, the details of which were accidentally lost or deliberately suppressed.

Hoftijzer (1958: 25–26) has shown that these points do not in of themselves indicate a new or different genealogy but can be reconciled with the biblical genealogy that shows Canaan to be Noah's grandson, fathered by Ham not *literally* the brother of Shem and Japheth. The statement "Ham the father of Canaan saw the nakedness of his father," gives basis for this interpretation. There are several instances in biblical writings in which the grandson is referred to as the son and this may be one of those occasions.

Felder (1989: 39–40) opted to find two independent stories in the text of Genesis 9:

> the original version of Genesis 9:18–27 only referred to Ham and his error [of *leaving* his father uncovered], and a later version of the story — one motivated by political developments in ancient Palestine — attempted to justify Shem's descendants (Israel) and those of Japheth (Philistines) over the subjugated Canaanites.

McDaniel (1992) offers an alternative approach to the curse of Canaan which recognizes the validity and unity of the Hebrew text as is with its seeming inconsistencies. For him this passage in its present form is narrative theology designed to explain the origin of sin after the flood. The inconsistencies are deliberate — they are the theologian's way of demonstrating that Noah spoke while still in a drunken stupor. He speaks incoherently while still under the influence of wine.

Whereas, in Genesis 1–3, sin was depicted as being born in an earthly rebellion against human limits in the attempt "to be like God," the "parable" of Noah's drunkenness in Genesis 9, according to McDaniel, tells of sin's earthly rebirth by an accident. Noah was the first viniculturalist. He had no experience with wine; consequently, his erratic exhibitionist behavior was unintentional and accidental. Nevertheless, sin became manifest — in Noah's behavior, not in Ham's or Canaan's behavior.

Noah sinned not only in getting drunk, but also in violating the social mores against exposing the pudendum, but also in his projection of responsibility for his embarrassing behavior. Ham did what any younger sibling would have done. He told his older brothers. It was certainly no sin for Ham to enter his father's tent; children had access to their parents. Ham had no way of knowing that his father was for the first time ever "out of control," thanks to new wine. Ham and his brothers together acted responsibly. For Ham not to have alerted his brothers would have been irresponsible, even for a junior sibling.

However, Noah still "under the influence", was incapable of thinking straight, incapable of assuming responsibility. Incoherently, he makes a curse in an effort to redeem the situation. But he only compounded the problem. With the curse on the wrong character, Canaan, (though Ham was equally innocent in the plain sense of the Hebrew text) victimization of the innocent was reintroduced. McDaniel (1992) notes, "whereas sin's curse outside Eden first expressed itself in fratricide (Cain's killing Abel), sin's curse from Noah's befouled mouth created slavery amongst brothers." Wine could not sweeten sin's new expression; it would prove to be as deadly as the old sin before the flood.

This concludes the survey of translations and interpretations of the "curse of Ham" or the "curse of Canaan." I am not prepared to agree with Rosenberg (cited above), that this story is "children's literature" or find "it as another instance of J's [the author's] humor." This is narrative theology at its best; but unfortunately its misapplication has had tragic consequences for millions of Blacks.

HAGAR THE EGYPTIAN HANDMAID

In dealing with Hagar, it is important that we do not follow this simple syllogism: Hagar was an Egyptian, Hagar was a slave, therefore Hagar was a Black. Such reasoning reinforces racist stereotyping. Since Egyptians in antiquity could be Negroid or Caucasian, it is quite possible that Hagar was Black. However, it cannot be argued that Hagar was Black because she was an Egyptian who was at the same time a slave. Slavery in Hagar's day was not controlled by race. As will be seen below, in Jewish tradition, Hagar was a daughter of the Pharaoh, given as a gift to Sarai, much like another Pharaoh gave a daughter to Solomon as a wife (I Kings 3:1).

Von Rad (1961: 189) made an indirect association of Ishmael with Africa in stating, "He will be a real Bedouin, a 'wild ass of a man' (*pere'*, zebra), i.e., free and wild (cf. Job 39:5–8), eagerly spending his life in a war of all against all—a worthy son of his rebellious and proud mother." The choice of "zebra" rather than "wild ass" suggests Africa, i.e., Black Africa, though this is far removed from Paran and the traditional desert domain of the Bedouin.

However, the "African" element here does not seem to be complimentary since Ishmael was again cited by von Rad (1961:191) as the one who was "free and rebellious, going forth to a battle of all against all." In fact, the Ishmaelites never were a match for the warring children of Isaac, Esau and Israel.[11]

According to Sarna (1989: 119) the name Hagar is probably related to the Arabic *hajara* meaning "to flee," suggesting that her name means "fugitive." If so the traditions in Genesis 16 and 21 tell why she was given that name or how it came to pass that she lived up to her name. (We should also keep in mind that Sarai and Sarah mean "Princess." It is a name and title of authority! In light of this, it is not surprising that God tells Abraham, "whatever the 'Princess' (Sarai) tells you to do, do as she says . . . .")

By way of understanding Sarai's giving Hagar to Abram as his "woman,"[12] it will be necessary to look at ancient Near Eastern

13

customs dealing with barrenness. Sarna (1989: 119) sets the context of Sarah's taking the initiative in using her handmaid in the following words:

> The custom of an infertile wife providing her husband with a concubine in order to bear children is well documented in the ancient Near East. The laws of Lipit-Ishtar (early 19th cent. B.C.E.) deal with the case of a harlot who produces children for the husband of a barren wife; these become his heirs. An Old Assyrian marriage contract (19th cent. B.C.E.) stipulates that if the wife does not provide him with an offspring within two years she must purchase a slave woman for the purpose.[13] The provision of a concubine slave for bearing children is taken for granted in the laws of Hammurabi in the specific case of a wife who is a priestess and is thus barred from giving birth.[14] In Sarai's case, it is unclear whether she had fully despaired of ever having children of her own or whether her action reflects the widespread popular belief that a woman who was unable to conceive may become fertile by adopting a child.

However, the concubine who provided the husband with a child was not to assume equality with the wife. If she did, as is clear from the Hammurabi law code (*ANET* 172: paragraphs 146–147), she was to be placed back among the ordinary slaves:

> When a seignior married a hierodule and she gave a female slave to her husband and she has then borne children, if later that female slave has claimed equality with her mistress because she bore children, her mistress may not sell her; she may mark her with the slave-mark and count her among the slaves. If she did not bear children, her mistress may sell her.

According to the older Ur-Nammu code (*ANET Supplement* 525) the insolent concubine was to have "her mouth scoured with one quart of salt." As von Rad (1961: 187) points out by calling attention to Proverbs 30:23, the competition between a maid and a mistress was one of three or four things that can make the earth tremble.

The Hammurabi law code protected the rights of the son of the slave under certain conditions. It stated:

> When a seignior's first wife bore him children and his female slave also bore him children, if the father during his lifetime has ever said "My children!" to the children whom the slave bore him, thus having counted them with the children of the first wife, after the father has gone to (his) fate, the children of the first wife and the children of the slave shall share equally in the goods of the paternal estate, with the first-born, the son of the first wife, receiving a preferential share.

However, if the father during his lifetime has never said "My children!" to the children whom the slave bore him, after the father has gone to (his) fate, the children of the slave may not share in the goods of the paternal estate along with the children of the first wife; freedom for the slave and her children shall be effected, with the children of the first wife having no claim against the children of the slave for service. (*ANET* 173: paragraphs 170–171)

We become indirectly aware of the presence of Hagar in Genesis 12:16 ("And for her [Sarai's] sake he dealt well with Abram; and he had sheep, oxen, male donkeys, male and female slaves, female donkeys, and camels"), although Hagar is not distinctly mentioned by name. It has been suggested by Tamez (1986: 6) that this event occurred during the third dynasty of Ur and the twelfth Egyptian dynasty,[15] but the meaning of the story does not depend on its date.

Ginzberg (1909, 223–224) has provided a summary of the expanded Jewish tradition about Abram's and Sarai's going to Egypt because a devastating famine consumed the land of Canaan where they lived. According to Jewish tradition, the breath taking beauty of Sarai, that exceeded even the beauty of Eve, overwhelmed the Pharaoh of Egypt and caused him *"to write a marriage contract"* (italics mine) giving to her all he owned of gold, silver, male and female slaves and the province of Goshen. The *"Pharaoh even gave his own daughter, Hagar, as a slave to Sarai"* (italics mine) rather than to have her reign as a mistress in some other harem.

According to this tradition —which here follows the biblical text— Pharaoh was not aware of the fact that Sarai was the wife of Abram and did not gain this knowledge until the plague of leprosy descended upon him and all his personal possessions. Terrorized by the plague, he sought for the cause of his affliction and learned that he was about to violate the wife of a chosen servant of God. In desperation he called for Abram, restored his untouched wife to him, bestowed upon him gifts of great value upon Abram, and ordered him to leave Egypt.

Thus, Hagar became the "handmaid" of Sarah, and it is important to note that she was not the concubine slave belonging to Abraham.[16] According to Tamez (1986: 6), Hebrew law repeatedly prohibited the abuse of servants and also stated that Hebrew solidarity extended only to the Hebrew people. For this reason, the Hebrews accepted or took for themselves only foreigners for bond-slaves because they did not want to subject fellow Israelites to the treatment attended to true slaves.[17]

Slaves could come from conquered nations, subdued and vanquished as a result of being defeated in war. These persons could gain a place of respect and endearment in the families who may have purchased them or acquired them through some arrangement with the army or the powers of government. There were other slaves that were bought and sold like common property on auction blocks or out of pens or in the market place. These people had lost personal dignity, the right to speak on their own behalf, whose physical bodies became a substitute for unpaid debts and who were totally without any recourse for they were poor, destitute, and struggling to survive.

Teubal (1990: 54) pointed out that,

> Since Hagar was given to Abraham *l'ishah* (as wife) but had only one pregnancy, it is feasible that a specific wedding ceremony took place sanctifying that particular occasion. This was not a marriage in the conventional sense of an alliance between families or clans. It would seem that Hagar was neither slave nor concubine nor conventional wife of Abraham. But she was the *shifhah* of Sarah. Nevertheless, because there is no term [in English] to fit this particular function, there is not reason to relate it to concubinage.

To all intents and purposes, Hagar was destined to remain the *shifh*ah "handmaid" of Sarai until Sarai died or unless Abram and Sarai wished to give her emancipation. In McDaniel's opinion (1992), what actually happened was a divorce in the literal sense of the word: Abraham "sent her away" (*weyĕšallĕhhā*, which is the technical term "to divorce her" in Hebrew).

Hagar's name is not prominently brought into play until the Genesis 16:1, which reads:

> Now Sarai, Abram's wife, had borne him no children, but she had an Egyptian maid-servant, also referred to as bond-servant, named Hagar; so she said to Abram, "the Lord has kept me from having children. Go, "sleep" with my maid-servant; perhaps I can build up (a family) through her.

According to Ginzberg, Sarai was willing to recognize her inability to bear children as her responsibility. Thus, without jealousy, she was willing to surrender her maid-servant to Abram. It is important to note that Hagar was not the property of Abram but she was the property of Sarai. We can assume that she was taught the Hebrew way of life, mannerisms, customs and beliefs by Sarai. Perhaps she was instructed in the religious beliefs and practices of the Hebrews by Sarai. Hagar was a suitable substitute for Sarai in the accepted practice of bearing children for her mistress.

The term "build up (a family)" suggests a child sired by Abram and Sarai, but Sarai was barren and a woman who had passed the child-bearing age (Genesis 18:11–12). It was Abram who believed that his heir would be a servant in his household rather than a child from his own body because he was an old man. God responded to him that Abram's heir would come from his own body (his seed), for He had said so.

Sarai became overwhelmed with the fact that she was barren. She conceived the idea to have Hagar function as the surrogate for her to bear Abram's child in line with the cultural and legal provisions of her time. This would give a male child born from the union of Hagar and Abram the full legal rights to Abram's inheritance. To her, this was the only solution to the major obstacle in fulfilling the promise God had made Abram.

If Abraham took another wife along with Sarah or in lieu of Sarah, a child born to the second *wife* would obviously be the child of that wife. However, there was the custom, noted above, that permitted the wife's slave or handmaid to be made pregnant by a woman's husband and the child would be considered the child of the *wife*, not the child of the maid or slave. When the child came forth out of the body of the slave, it would be received on the upper legs of the barren woman and thus the barren woman could claim the off-spring as her child.[18] This was a common practice by the people in this geographical area.

Because Hagar became the mother of Abram's first borne son, the stigma that was experienced by Sarai because of her barrenness actually became a blessing to Hagar. The baby borne by Hagar was a son of promise. However, the biological mother was a slave and a foreigner.

Sarai was not prepared for the consequences that ensued. Ishmael, though refused and detested by Sarai, became one of the many first-born sons in Israelite-Jewish tradition and history who was supplanted by a second son of the same father.[19]

Hagar, no doubt, as the handmaid to Sarah relished the possibility of her becoming elevated to an exalted level in the social order by bearing the son of a wealthy, influential, chosen vessel of God. This pregnancy gave her the opportunity to be lifted in the eyes of others. She was able to accomplish what her mistress could not do. God had smiled on her and granted her a choice gift. A child fathered by Abram was growing within her. Hopefully, it would be a male child who would garner for her a place of honor, respect, and love in the household.

Sarai's recourse to her culture's solution for barrenness, had granted to Hagar possibilities of great import. However, this dream of personal exaltation and the attended creature comforts were short-lived. The fulfillment of Hagar's imagined place of importance in Abram's household never became a reality. Hagar's imagined ascendancy in the eyes of her lord and her delightful demise of her mistress's situation could no longer be subdued.

Sarai's remarks to Hagar were not subtle, her words were sharp, her hatred of Hagar became vitriolic. Hackett (1989: 14) noted that the Hebrew word that is translated "dealt hardly or oppressed" carries the connotation of physical harm. As Speiser (1964: 117) indicated, Sarai became physically, as well as verbally, abusive to Hagar.

Sarai demonstrated another indication of human weakness. Like Adam and Eve, she transfers the blame from herself to another person. She did not say, "I was wrong to do what other women do." Rather, Sarai said to Abram, "You are responsible for the wrong I am suffering. I put my servant in your arms, and now that she knows that she is pregnant, she despises me. May the Lord judge between you and me." (This difficulty would never have occurred if Sarai had let God work out His plan.)

Abram's response was, "Your servant is in your hands, do with her what you think best." The text continues, "Then Sarai mistreated Hagar; so she fled from her." Gunkel, cited by von Rad (1961: 187), stated that Abram "plays an unhappy role between these two headstrong women." Gunkel referred to Sarai as "the contentious wife." Skinner (1930: 286) analyzed Sarai's outburst, "My wrong be upon thee!" as "her injured self-respect finding vent in a passionate and most unjust imprecation."

Sarai's unreasoning and caustic outburst may be due to the fact that the near eastern social standard jeopardizes Sarai's status to the point that she may lose the honored position as a wealthy pastoral chief's wife until she is able to give birth to male offspring. Hackett suggested that Hagar was "defiant", Sarai is passionate and raging and Abram was situated between them. Sarai's statement places the blame of the whole scenario on Abram as if he was the one responsible for the way Hagar was acting since he made her pregnant.

The statement that Sarai makes to Abram almost sounds like an echo from the expression of Laban to Jacob, "The Lord watch between me and thee while we are absent one from another" (Genesis 31:49). The response of Abram suggests that the episode between him and Hagar was without feeling, without tenderness, without concern.

The situation in the tent of Abram as far as Hagar was concerned was more than she could tolerate mentally, verbally, emotionally, and physically. She left the place where she has been staying with her master and mistress and fled in the direction of her homeland. Angry, frustrated, with tears and mounting stress she left the place that she had known for many years with the feeling of release. While in the wilderness the angel of the Lord[20] spoke to her. This was a unique situation for this was the first time in the Genesis that the angel of the Lord tells a woman to return to the place from which she has fled seeking, emotional and physical peace. It is the second time in Genesis that Yahweh converses with a woman.

The second thing of note is that this was the first time that the angel of the Lord made a promise that involved Hagar's offspring and genealogy. Thirdly, this is the second time that the name of a child to be borne is enunciated by the angel of the Lord. (This is one of six names so declared prior to the birth of the child and the name of this child is Ishmael.)

Some scholars state that Yahweh spoke to her rather than His messenger as is seen in other passages of scripture. This is supported by the name by which Hagar addresses the Divine, namely 'ēl ra'î "God who sees (me)" and laḥay ro'î "the Living One who sees me."

To the uninitiated the message of the angel seems cruel and without feeling. Surely, Yahweh is cognizant of the abuse that Hagar has received from the hand of Sarai and its mounting intensity that has forced her to leave the place she has known as home for so many years. Why is it that Sarai is not punished? Why is not something done to alleviate the hostility between these two women that burns within the confines of that tent? No, she is told to return back to

Sarai and to submit herself again to the abuse from which she has fled.

The only note of aggrandizement promised her is that her descendants will be "greatly multiplied," they will be of great number. This is conveyed to Hagar in a way that is typical of the Genesis tradition that is found in the promises made to the patriarchal fathers. The unique feature is that this promise is not made to a man but to a woman, a daughter of Egypt, the handmaid of Sarai.

In Genesis 21, the names of Sarai and Abram were changed to Sarah and Abraham after which Sarah became fertile, pregnant, and bore Isaac. Abraham was 100 years old when his son was born. When the child was eight days old, Abraham circumcised him. The child grew and when he was weaned a great feast was held marking the event. Sarah saw Ishmael playing with Isaac and demanded Abraham to "get rid of that slave woman and her son, for that slave woman's son will never share the inheritance with my son Isaac."

This demand of Abraham required Hagar and Ishmael to leave the home of the patriarch. Sarah's fear was registered in her words: she did not wish Ishmael to have any part in sharing Abraham's inheritance with Isaac. This was a mark of fearful insecurity. Once again, she was interfering with God's plan for both boys. Abraham responded to her request but he registered personal concern in executing her demand. Abraham seemed to be worried to some extent about the welfare of his first-born son, but not his son's mother. According to the biblical writer, the spirit of God spoke to him, encouraging him to follow Sarah's request, as well as informing him that no harm would come to Ishmael.

In Genesis 21:13, God said, "I will make the son of the bond-woman a nation because he is thy seed." This was a divine promise from Yahweh that corroborated the same promise that God made to Hagar in the wilderness. Sarna noted, the legal position of Ishmael is quite clear:

Sarah had undertaken to recognize as her own the male offspring of the union of Abraham with Hagar, a match that she herself had initiated and imposed on her husband (16:2). Abraham, for his part, undoubtedly recognized Ishmael as his legitimate son, a fact repeatedly attested by a variety of earlier texts (16:15; 17:23, 25f.) and affirmed here (v. 11) as well as later on (25:9, 12).

Sarna asked the rhetorical question, "Did this status assure Ishmael automatic inheritance rights even after the birth of Isaac?" He answered with an emphatic affirmative:

> The laws of Hammurabi (par. 170f. [cited above]) and of the still earlier Lipit-Ishtar (par. 25 [cited above]) implicitly make inheritance rights a legal consequence of a father's acceptance of the infant as his legitimate son. There is no doubt that Ishmael was entitled to a share of Abraham's estate. The key to Sarah's demand lies in a clause in the laws of the Lipit-Ishtar where it is stipulated that the father may grant freedom to the slave woman and the children she has borne him, in which case they forfeit their share of the paternal property (cf. Judg. 11:1-3). Sarah is asking Abraham to exercise that legal right (cf. 25:6).

Early the next morning the infant Ishmael and Hagar, his mother, moved off into the desert toward Beersheba. Abraham gave them only a skin of water and a loaf of bread.

In *The Methodist Quarterly Review* (July–August, 1895), it was stated that some commentators concluded from Genesis 21:14 that Abraham preceded with singleness of heart and with a feeling of self-denial in dismissing the mother and son from his home. This was done by some writers to force out of the scriptural record something creditable to Abraham. But if we picture Hagar blind with tears, stinging from the sense of the cruel wrong that was heaped upon her, her heart full of fear and apprehension as to what might befall her and the young lad wandering in the desert, we can see little to commend in Abraham's actions.

As desperate as the situation was, God intervened and delivered the infant Ishmael from the hand of death. He responded to the cry of Ishmael and the prayer of Hagar and showed them a way of passage through the impossible situation that confronted them both alone there in the desert. He promised Hagar that Ishmael would be the father of a great nation.

A part of this great nation coming from Ishmael bears the name of Hagar, namely, the Hagarites. In Ps 83:7 the Hagarites of Moab are mentioned *along with* the Ishmaelites of Edom. In 1 Chron 5:10, 19-23, the Hagarites are mentioned as being the victims of king Saul's warfare and the forces of the Reubenites, the Gadites, and the half-tribe of Manasseh. Assuming there was a connection between Hagar and the Hagarites, as well as the Hagarites and the Ishmaelites (two sons of Ishmael are Hagarites according to Gen 25:15 and 1 Chron 5:19), the legacy of Cain's fratricide and Noah's enslaving his children followed into Israel's "Golden Age" when "war was of God" (1 Chron 5:22).

But as Sarna (1989: 122) pointed out with specific reference to Ishmael and the Hagarites:

> It is noteworthy that the image of Ishmael in the Bible, as distinct from later Jewish literature, is by and large not a negative one. He is not an inveterate enemy of Israel. In fact there seems to have been some intermingling between the tribe of Simeon and the Ishmaelites, for the clans of Mibsam and Mishma are associated with both, as proved by Genesis 25:13 and 1 Chronicles 4:25. The Ishmaelites do not appear among the victims of David's raids into the south lands, even though these incursions encroached upon their habitat, as is clear from 1 Samuel 27:8 and Genesis 25:18. David's sister married "Jether the Ishmaelite," according to 1 Chronicles 2:17, and among the administrators of crown property under David were "Obil the Ishmaelite" and "Jaziz the Hagarite," according to 1 Chronicles 27:30f.

MOSES' CUSHITE WIFE

The biblical literature speaks clearly of Moses marriage to Zipporah, one of Reuel's seven daughters:

The priest of Midian had seven daughters . . . [and] when they returned to their father Reuel, he said, "How is it that you have come back so soon today?" They said, "An Egyptian helped us against the shepherds; he even drew water for us and watered the flock. He said to his daughters, "Where is he? Why did you leave the man? Invite him to break bread." Moses' agreed to stay with the man, and he gave Moses his daughter Zipporah in marriage." (Exodus 2:17–21)

Josephus (*Antiquities* XI: 1) spoke of this marriage also. He noted:

Moses', thinking it would be a terrible reproach upon him if he overlooked the young women under unjust oppression [from the shepherds], and should suffer the violence of the men to prevail over the right of the maidens, he drove away the men, who had a mind to more than their share, and afforded a proper assistance to the women. . . . Now the father took well from his daughters that they were so desirous to reward their benefactor, and he bid them to bring Moses into his presence. . . . So he made him his son, and gave him one of his daughters in marriage, and appointed him to the guardian and superintendent over his cattle.[21]

However, this is the second marriage of Moses according to Josephus. In *Antiquities* X, Josephus had already discussed Moses's marriage to the Ethiopian princess Tharbis. He wrote as follows concerning the termination of Moses' campaign against the Ethiopians:

He came upon the Ethiopians before they had expected him; and joining battle with them he beat them . . . indeed made a great slaughter of these Ethiopians. Now when the Egyptian army had tasted of this prosperous success, by means of Moses, they did not slacken their diligence, insomuch that the Ethiopians were in danger of being reduced to slavery, and all sorts of destruction; and at length they retired to Saba, which was a royal city of Ethiopia, which [the persian King] Cambyses afterwards [sixth century B. C.] named Merōe, after the name of his own sister. The place was to be besieged with very great difficulty . . . being encompassed with a

23

strong wall, and having the river to guard them from their enemies, and having great ramparts between the wall and rivers . . .

However, while Moses was uneasy at the army's lying idle (for the enemy durst not come to a battle), this accident happened: Tharbis was the daughter of the king of the Ethiopians. She happened to see Moses as he led the army near the walls, and fought with great courage; and admiring the subtlety of his undertakings . . . she fell deeply in love with him; and upon the prevalence of that passion, set to him the most faithful of all her servants to discourse with him about their marriage. He thereupon accepted the offer, on condition she would procure the delivering up of the city, and gave her the assurance of an oath to take her to his wife; and that once he had taken possession of the city, he would not break his oath to her. No sooner was the agreement made, but it took effect immediately; and when Moses had cut off the Ethiopians, he gave thanks to God, and consummated his marriage, and led the Egyptians back to their own land.

The witness of Josephus notwithstanding, there is for some scholars uncertainty about how many wives Moses had and about the meaning of Cush in these traditions. According to Albright (1941: 34, note 8), the Egyptian Execration texts from the nineteenth century B. C. cite *Kushu* as a place name probably "in the region of the Arnon south-ward into Midian, corresponding to the archaic Kushan of Hab. 3:7, which appears as a synonym for Midian." Albright (1968: 205, note 49) recognized this as a tentative identification. However, Cross (1973: 204), citing Albright, made the identification definite and concluded:

The term *Kūš* originally applied to an element in the Midianite league, a name elsewhere used of a south Transjordanian district alongside the by-form *Kūšān*. *There is thus no reason to suppose that the Cushite wife is not also the Zipporah of the Yahwistic tradition* [italics mine]. The term "Cushite" may also have had connotation of blackness derived from its homonym, "Ethiopian," rendering the whitened skin of Miriam a singularly fit punishment for her objections to the Cushite wife.[22]

Most commentators, however, recognize two wives: one Midianite and one Cushite (Ethiopian). According to Milgrom (1990: 93),

Those who claim that Cush is Ethiopia clearly cannot identify the woman with Zipporah. They cite an elaborate legend of how Moses had married an Ethiopian. Others, however, place Cush in Midianite territory (Hab. 3:7) or understand Cushite as an adjective meaning beautiful [*Targum Onkeles*, *Targum Jerusalmi*, and *Sifre* on Numbers, 99], thus allowing for the identification with Zipporah. That the marriage with Zipporah, consummated so much earlier (Exod. 2:21), would cause such a belated shock can be explained by the fact that her husband had left her behind when he went to Egypt to redeem his people, and she only rejoined him at Sinai, to be seen for the first time by the Israelites (Exod. 18:5–6).

Regardless of whether Moses' wife was Ethiopian or Midianite, the objection to her, it is implied was ethnic (cf. Lev. 24:10). Strikingly, the rabbis raised no objection to her Cushite origin but, to the contrary, defend her, claiming that Moses refused to have sexual intercourse after his descent from Sinai.

According to Milgrom (1990: 97), Miriam's punishment was leprosy that made her as "scaly as snow":

Leprosy was considered a punishment for offenses against the Deity in Israel (and elsewhere in the ancient Near East). According to the rabbis, the chief cause for leprosy is defamation, interpreting *metsor'* as *motsi' shem ra'*, "slander." If Cushite means Ethiopian then the whiteness of Miriam would be a fit punishment for objecting to Moses' dark-skinned wife. However the simile of snow indicates the flakiness associated with the disease, not whiteness (cf. Pss 68:15; 147:16).[23]

Adamo (1986:121) listed eight reasons for not identifying Moses' Cushite wife with the Kushanite/Midianites or the Kassites. They are in summary as follows: (1) the texts do not equate Zipporah and the Cushite; (2) Miriam could hardly be addressing a marriage that Moses entered into years earlier; (3) Midian does not equal Cush and Midianite does not equal Cushite as shown by the fact that Jethro was never called a Cushite; (4) the wording of Numbers 12:1 suggest a recent marriage; (5) Cush when defined in the Bible always refers to Ethiopia; (6) the proverbial beauty of the Cushites led to the word Cush taking on the meaning of beauty; (7) Targum Jonathan made the Cushite wife the queen of Ethiopia; and (8) Josephus [cited above] gave a detailed account of the encounter of Moses with the Cushite Tharbis.

Over against this evidence, efforts to make Moses a monogamist seem empty. Assertions, like "Moses married a descendent of the son of Abraham and not a member of the Negro race," found in Dake's notes (cited by Adamo 1986: 121) seem weak in light of Jewish tradition.

THE QUEEN OF SHEBA

For many centuries in Christian, Jewish, or Muslim history, the Queen of Sheba was considered a mythic figure from the southern part of Arabia. There was also the suggestion among Western scholars of note that she was not a Black woman of African descent.

The earliest mention of Ethiopia in the Bible is, as Felder (1989: 10) noted, found in Genesis 2:13 which we understand is a part of the older version dealing with the creation by "J", dated around 950 B.C. The writer of this tradition referred to the River Gihon "which flows around the whole land of *Cush* [King James Version *Ethiopia*]" which encircled part of biblical Eden. The River Gihon was not given an exact physical location in the geography of the scriptures. However, Westermann (1984) stated "Cush is mainly Ethiopia or Nubia, the land south of Egypt, or more exactly the area between the first and fourth cataract of the Nile." In Genesis 10:7, the name Gihon, is given to one of the sons of Cush. It is possible that the River Gihon refers to the Nile River.

However, in McDaniel's opinion (1992) Hamblin (1987: 132–133) has provided a good case for identifying both the Gihon and the Pishon with ancient rivers that intersected with the Tigris/Euphrates confluence just before they enter the Persian Gulf. If this is so, then the *Cush* in Genesis 2:13 would more likely be a reference to the Mesopotamian Kassites than to the Ethiopians.

Hamblin's evidence comes from the work of Juris Zarins who has worked for seven years on his hypothesis that the garden of Eden lies submerged in the Persian Gulf. Satellite photography reveal "fossil rivers" through northern Arabia and the dry river beds known as Wadi Rimah and Wadi Batin. The Wadi Batin, Zarins believes, was the River Pishon and the River Gihon is the present Karun River which flows for about 515 miles into the Shatt-al-Arab and the Persian Gulf.[24]

References to Cush are many in the Old Testament and there are times when Egypt and Ethiopia are joined, emphasizing the greatness of each country. Egypt and Ethiopia were formative military powers great enough to counteract the hope of Judah against the Assyrian military conflict. The wealth of Egypt and Ethiopia are emphasized in Isaiah 45:14, and Nahum 3 also brings to our attention the strength of Ethiopia and Egypt. Observing Genesis 10, one comes to the conclusion that we are not dealing here with a single record of genealogy but rather a blending of the Yahwist and the priestly list from a redactor. It is also in this chapter that we note Seba and Sheba are mentioned as descendants of Ham. Genesis 10 also brings to our knowledge that two of Cush's descendants were called Sheba. Felder (1989: 24) noted, "The Bible's ambivalence about the location of the tribes of Sheba is similar to the ambivalence we find in some classical literature about the people called Ethiopians." Classical literature employs the term Ethiopian to refer to Black people who lived in Africa, south of Egypt. In some Greek writings the words Ethiopians refer to people who lived on the two shores of the Red Sea. The Greek author Strabo stated:

> In the case of the Ethiopians that "sundered in twain" [means]...[they] extend along the whole seaboard of Oceanus . . . . For the Ethiopians that are spoken of in this sense are "sundered in twain" naturally by the Arabian Gulf [the Red Sea]...as by a river [like Egypt by the Nile].[25]

Strabo stated that the Arabian Gulf was the natural boundary of division used by other writers who described geography to separate Africa from Asia. He further noted that,

> Homer divides the Ethiopians into two groups . . . not because he knew that the Indians were physically similar to the Ethiopians [for Homer probably did not know of the Indians at all...], but rather on the basis of the division of which I have spoken above . . . and that . . . the Ethiopians that border on Egypt are themselves, also, divided into two groups; for some of them live in Asia, others in Libya [Africa] though they differ in no respect from each other.

There is no concrete evidence from any source to establish that South Arabia ever ruled Ethiopia, in contradiction to Conti Rossini's assumptions. History reveals that South Arabia was under the domination of Ethiopia from about A.B. 334–370 and from A.D. 525–575. Felder (1989:26) noted that some believe that Ethiopia introduced Christianity to South Arabia through the missionary efforts of Tewoflos, despite the fact that Haenchen proposes and earlier date.

In the later period, the north section of the Marib Dam was constructed with headers protruding beyond the face of the wall. Gus Van Beek states that,

> This technique has no construction antecedents in South Arabian architecture. In Ethiopian architecture, on the other hand, the ends of wooden joists frequently protruded beyond the face of the building . . . and often done also in stone. In view of the fact that Ethiopians dominated Sabaeans throughout much of this period, it seems likely that they are also responsible for such architectural forms . . . this technique as cultural influence coming from Ethiopia to South Arabia.[26]

Felder indicated that some historians have used the biblical story of Queen of Sheba as valid proof of the precedence of South Arabia over the country of Ethiopia. Sheba has been associated with the country of Egypt and Nubia; (Isaiah 43:3) but it is now possible that Seba was located in Africa.[27] Genesis 10:28 lists Sheba among the sons of Shem; and in Genesis 25:3, Sheba is mentioned in the genealogy of Abraham and Keturah. These later references suggest that the Sabeans are relatives of the people who inhabited the Fertile Crescent and Arabia.

This means that the genealogical references show that the Israelites through the Sabeans were related to the people of the Fertile Crescent —including themselves —on the one hand, and to the people of Africa on the other. The south Arabian and early Ethiopian histories developed by Glaser and Conti Rossini seemed to substantiate the southern Arabian influence on Ethiopian culture. This was because of the importance that was attached to the name *Hbst* that was seen on a large number of the Sabean text. Irvine (1985: 181), a critic of Conti Rossini, whom Felder quoted, had this to say about the *Hbst*:

> By a process of conquest of absorption [the habashat] merged with the local native Hamitic population and became 'Africanized'. From this source arose the proto-Ethiopian civilization and the proto-Ethiopic text of Ethiopia.

It is out of this background that Makeda, the Queen of Sheba emerges.

Historians, poets, playwrights, and explorers have been captivated by the name of *Makeda*, the legendary Queen of Sheba. There are many fragmentary bits of information concerning this legendary Queen, who in southern Arabia is called *Belkis*. The following nine pages provide a summary of important details coming from the legend.

The earliest extant form of the Queen of Sheba narrative is preserved in I Kings 10:1–13 and II Chronicles 9:1–12. These references have some small but insignificant differences in the account. Ullendorff (1962–1963: 486–501) pointed to considerable interest in the transmission of the two texts. Josephus addressed her as the Queen of Egypt and Ethiopia.

Queen Makeda was an outstanding administrator, builder, and international stateswoman whose life demonstrates that monarchy can co-exist side by side in Africa with patriarchy. The dynasty with which she is identified in Ethiopia was established in 1370 B. C. instituted by Za Besi Anganbo lasting for 350 years. Makeda's father and grandfather were the last two male rulers of this dynasty. When her brother, Prince Noural, died at an early age, Princess Makeda inherited her fathers throne.

Queen Makeda, according to Yeschaq (1989: 5–11), was born in Tigre Province and was the daughter of very wealthy parents who descended from a very powerful people. She was trained in and acquired a formidable knowledge of natural history, music and astronomy. She was a most unusual woman and for her lifetime had been interested in questioning the mysteries of life and was also very well acquainted with the rituals of the Temple. Instructed and guided in the arts, the crafts, the skills, and the affairs of State, aptly tutored by Queen Ismenie, her mother, she developed into the role of a strong ruling Queen of Ethiopia.

In the year 1005 B. C., from his death bed, her father appointed her to succeed him. History will attest that for fifty years she ruled her country with justice, fortitude, and wisdom. Traditions, cited by Baldwin (1874: 61), credit her with governing an extensive area of land that included parts of upper Egypt, Ethiopia, parts of Arabia, Syria, Armenia, India and the entire area between the Mediterranean and Erythraean Sea. The seat of her authority and power was later known as Axum. The Yemenite kingdom of Himyarite acknowledged her suzerainty.

Margaret Shinnie (1968: 30) compiling historical data of the inhabitants of Axum stated,

The most powerful of Kush's neighbors were the Axumited, people from the southern tip of Arabia who had settled across the sea from their homeland and made a kingdom on the western Coast of the Red Sea-the Kingdom of Axum.

Arnold Heeren, a 19th century author cited by Baldwin (1874), confidently declared that the Ethiopians of Arabia gained extensive control in India and may have settled on the coast of Hindustan. Makeda ruled over a substantial empire exercising her absolute rule over many far-flung lands in her kingdom.

Makeda, as an administrator and business person, engaged in extensive trade all over the then known world to ensure her countries economical survival and to enhance her status as a world leader. She was astute as a commercial trader and demonstrated this by the boldness of her trade relations in the markets of Damascus and Gaza. Her trade network was organized to include both land and sea investments and was very effectively manned by shrewd and watchful Ethiopian merchants.

The leader of this merchant organization was Tamrin, described in the *Kebra Nagast* (*The Glory of the Ethiopian Kings*) was a seer and man of great wisdom.[28] As evidence of his fantastic expertise at business involvement of import and export, he utilized 520 camels and 370 vessels laden with great wealth of gold and silver from the empire of Queen Makeda. This would be equivalent to the Merchant Marines business enterprise of a major world power on today's scale of global commerce.

About this time King Solomon of Jerusalem was building the Temple of God and his Navy was roaming the Red Sea Coast in search of gold in Ophir and wood for the pillars of the Temple and for his palace. Hearing about this popular merchant, Solomon enlisted the services of Tamrin along with other merchants to supply materials for these great structures. Tamrin brought to Solomon, in Jerusalem, gold, silver, precious stones and black lumber from Ethiopia. Ezekiel 27:22–24 gives an apt description of her merchants.

The merchants of Sheba and Raamah were thy merchants; they traded in thy fairs with the best of all spices, and with all precious stones, and gold. Haran, and Canneh, and Eden, the merchants of Sheba, Asshur, and Chilmad were thy merchants. These were thy merchants in all sorts of things, in blue clothes, and embroidered work, and in chests of rich apparel, bound with cords, and made of cedar, among thy merchandise.

It is possible, according to Wendt (1962: 109), that because of her extensive trade routes there was even in 985 B. C. a Chinese expedition to the land of Sheba; but there is no documented proof of the extremes of her commercial exploits.

In the *Book of Axum*, it is written that Makeda erected her capital in the district of Azeba when she ascended the throne of Ethiopia. The *Kebra Nagast* stated that she erected her capital at Debra Makeda or "Mount Makeda." Clarke (1978: vi) stated that "Debra Makeda later became a meeting place for the early Christians of Ethiopia." Baldwin (1874: 85) had this to say about one of the building projects of capital Belkis-Makeda:

> Hamzas of Isphan says: "The Himyarites relate that Belkis, having become Queen, built in Saba the dike called Arim. The other inhabitants of Yemen dispute this, and maintain that the dike Arim was constructed by Lokman, the second son of Ad: and they say that time having brought it to a condition of decay, Belkis, on becoming Queen, repaired the damage it had suffered."

That which provokes our greatest interest and curiosity pivots around her legendary visit to King Solomon, the third King of Israel. Some items of import concern the romantic interlude that involved these two monarchs. Queen Makeda's interest in King Solomon was provoked by the fascinating things that she heard from her merchant representative,
Tamrin. To negotiate a trade contract with King Solomon provided the reason for her visit to Jerusalem, because he may have wielded some influence over trade routes important to the Sabaeans.

If the speculations regarding the extent and scope of her empire are valid we can rest assure that she exercised control over far more important kingdom than did Solomon. I Kings 10 and II Chronicles 9 give us the biblical backdrop for her visit. The scripture states that (Makeda) the queen of Sheba, "came to test him with hard questions" which very easily may have concerned political, diplomatic, or commercial problems to prove his wisdom. We are told in I Kings 10:2 that "she talked with him about all that was within her heart."

It was suggested by Ullendorff, that the two Hebrew expressions in particular which appear to imply a union of King Solomon and the Queen, either marriage or possibly concubinage were, "the Queen came to Solomon and communed with him all that was in her heart," found in I Kings 10:2. The Hebrew verb "to come, to enter," was also used for coitus, as in Genesis 16:2.

There may have been administrative problems that were difficult to resolve that she needed to have satisfied by drawing on his experience as the ruler of Israel. According to today's monetary values, the 120 talents of gold given by Solomon to Makeda could be considered as a diplomatic or a commercial settlement. King Solomon honored her in a manner that recognized her prestige and influence. As Archbishop Yeschaq reports (1989: 5-11) the extrabiblical tradition, she resided as his guest in an apartment built of crystal that extended from the floor to the ceiling as her temporary residence. A throne was erected beside his covered with silk fringes, gold and silver studded with diamonds and pearls. He lavished upon her fantastic feasts in huge rooms, perfumed with fragrant incense and myrrh.

The Ethiopian *Kebra Nagast* (that contains the Sheba cycle in chapter 21) elucidates other significant changes worthy of consideration, e.g. no mention is made of the Queens hairy legs, nothing about the glass floor, or Sheba's involvement with demons.

Chapter 28 of the *Kebra Nagast* supplies many embellishments concerning the Queen's visit to Solomon that lead up to her giving birth to Menelik. Solomon had a fabulous banquet with sumptuous foods, highly seasoned that would provoke thirst and a desire for water. When the evenings festivities climaxed, King Solomon invited the Queen of Sheba to repose for the night and slumber in his palatial chambers. After much reflection, weighing the invitation, and the wisdom of accepting the same, the Queen agreed on one specific condition to rest for the night in the King's chambers. The condition was that King Solomon would not force himself upon her. To this request, he swore.

The King having complied with her sole condition, countered by making the Queen of Sheba promise not to take anything in the King's house, to which she promised to comply. Solomon climbed upon his couch for the nights repose on one side of the chamber and on the opposite side of the chamber her bed had been prepared. Near her bed he had placed a bowl of water. Early in the night Sheba awoke; the highly seasoned food had intensified her thirst, and she arose to satisfy this intense desire. As she arose to quench her thirst, Solomon seized her hands and accused her of breaching her oath.

Then he took advantage of her vulnerability, working his will against her helpless need.

It is stated that the King had a dream in which the *Shekinah* of God, a superlatively brilliant light representing the divine presence, had withdrawn from Israel and settled in Ethiopia.

Solomon was emotionally inflamed by this daughter of Africa that a romantic interlude ensued that led to the birth of their son, Menelik; he became the first King of Ethiopia of the line of Solomon. Queen Makeda satisfied her visit to Jerusalem as recorded in II Chronicles 9:12, "King Solomon gave to the Queen of Sheba all her desires, whatever she asked, beside what she had brought to the King."

Ullendorff suggested that the two versions of the Queen of Sheba story in I Kings and II Chronicles might have been interrupted to bring to our attention the cargo of gold, precious stones, and wood suitable for the fabrication of musical instruments that was conveyed by the Ophir fleet. The mention of these commercial activities in the southern Red Sea confirms and supports the historical account of the Queen of Sheba's visit to King Solomon.[29] Queen Makeda, according to Yeschaq, stayed in Jerusalem for six months, and on her journey back to Ethiopia she gave birth to her son Menelik I. "So she turned and went her way to her own land, she and her servants."

It is quite possible that along with the other agreements that were made a military alliance might have been included. The Queen ruled Ethiopia and all the territory subjected thereto and abdicated the throne in favor of her son, Menelik; however, she remained his advisor until death in 955 B. C.

Among the ancient Arabs it is not uncommon for Queens to sit in authority over a nation; and, as a result, we have no reason to question the genuineness of the biblical tradition. Cuneiform records list the names of many North Arabian Queens. According to Pritchard (1974: 283) no South Arabian inscriptions, however, have to date been discovered that refer to the Queen of Sheba or any Sabean ruler prior to 800 B. C.

Archaeological evidence found in Axum confirms the fact that the worship of the sun and worship of the serpent was a very popular religious practice in Ethiopia during the reign of the Queen of Sheba. This is validated by an engraving of a serpent on an upright sculptured stone in Axum. The description in Avesta, the sacred book of

Persia that involves the worship of serpents, is identical with the tradition found in Ethiopia. It is believed according to Selassie (1970: 4) that this religious practice invaded the land of Ethiopia.

The true worship of the God of Israel was officially introduced while Makeda was Queen of Ethiopia. She is credited with a mass reformation of religious worship in Ethiopia. According to the *Kebra Nagast*, when her son, Menelik I, visited his father, King Solomon, he returned to Ethiopia bringing the Ark of the Covenant in the company of Azaris who was the son of Zadok, the high priest, and the eldest sons of the house of Israel.[30]

When the Ark of the Covenant was brought to Ethiopia Queen Makeda prostrated herself, magnifying God Almighty, the one the Ark symbolized. A great celebration, no doubt a dedication, ensued after the worship of the Queen. The worship of God was then officially established in Ethiopia and Queen Makeda abdicated the throne in preference to her son and Solomon's son, Menelik I, who was then crowned King of Kings. For 3,000 years this family perpetuated itself until the deposing of Haile Selassie in 1947.

BLACK AND BEAUTIFUL

In the King James version, Song of Solomon 1:5 reads, in part "I am black, but comely . . . ." Without the benefit of seeing the verb forms in the Hebrew original, which do distinguish gender, and without recognizing that the speaker of verse five is the same person speaking in verse four being taken into the king's chambers, one would probably assume that these words were spoken by Solomon. But the truth of the matter is that these words were spoken by the Shulammite/Shunamite woman (Song of Songs 6:13)[31] who was deeply in love.

According to Pope (1977: 307), whose extensive and excellent commentary in the *Anchor Bible* on the Song of Songs has been used heavily in the preparation of the following material, efforts were made by Christian expositors to change the term *nigra* "black" to *fusca* "dark" and to use the word "but" in place of "and." The Septuagint here can be translated, "Black I am and beautiful." The Revised version changed the "black" of the King James version to "very dark," and in the succeeding verse softened the intensity of the word "black" to "swarthy."

Pope noted that in some biblical texts blackness is the "antithesis of beauty . . . since bodily health and beauty are described in the scriptures as white and ready" (as in Lam 4:7 and Song of Songs 5:10). This would imply that beauty and the absence of disease would be identified with whiteness or ruddiness — for people for whom white was the norm — and if there was any color other than white involved, it would have to be ruddy skin color.

Rashi, cited by Pope (1977: 308), seemly had a problem conceiving that the woman speaking in 1:5 could be both black *and* beautiful. He referred to her limbs as being beautiful and shapely despite the fact that they were black. He seems to have thought that her blackness would change to white if she remained in the shade for awhile. Pope noted that this is a reflection upon Rashi's lack of knowledge concerning the materials out of which the Bedouin tents are made, which is mentioned in the synonymous parallelism. These tents are made out of black goat hair that does not become white even if washed.

It is also interesting to note that Miriam and Aaron chastised Moses for marrying a Cushite woman, Numbers 12:1. Yahweh responded on Moses' behalf in anger against the brother and sister of Moses by smiting Miriam with leprosy that made her white with the disease for seven days, although Aaron received no punishment.[32]

Origen's treatment, Pope notes, reflects the melainophopia of traditional Christian and Jewish interpretations. He considered the beloved woman in this song to be the Bride of Christ, the Church gathered from among the Gentiles. For Origen, "the daughters of Jerusalem," whom she addresses, represented the Synagogue, looked upon with favor "because of the election of the [biblical patriarchal] Fathers" who were "nevertheless enemies of the gospel" of Jesus Christ.

For Origen, "the Synagogue vilifies the Church of the Gentiles for her ignoble birth, calling her black." The Church retaliates by saying:

I am indeed black, O daughters of Jerusalem, in that I cannot claim descent from famous men, nor have I received the enlightenment of Moses' Law. But I have my own beauty. For in me too is that primal thing, the Image of God in which I was created. You compare me to the tents of Qedar and the curtains of Solomon because of my dark coloring; but even Qedar was descended from Ishmael, as his second son, and Ishmael was not without his share in the divine blessing (cf. Gen. 25:13 and 16:11). You liken me to Solomon's curtains which are none other than the curtains of the Tabernacle of God (Exod 25:2ff). I am indeed surprised, O daughters of Jerusalem, that you should want to reproach me with the blackness of my hue. How could you forget what is written in your Law as to what Mary (Miriam) suffered who spoke against Moses because he had taken a black Ethiopian to wife? (Numbers 12). How is it that you do not recognize the true fulfillment of that type in me? I am that Ethiopian. I am indeed black by reason of my lowly origin; but I am beautiful through penitence and faith. (Pope 1977: 309)

This attitude of Origen regarding blackness is more negative than positive.

According to Pope, Origen, in discussing the Gentile Church, that designates itself as "Black but Beautiful,"
examined other segments of the scriptures that address Blacks and blackness in the Bible. These passages include the story of Solomon and the Queen of Sheba, allusions to Ethiopia in various texts, and the Ethiopian Ebed-Melek (Jer. 38 and 39). Origen explains the

incident dealing with Moses' marriage to the Ethiopian woman in ways that are mystical, yet positive. He suggested that the spiritual law, represented by Moses, merged with the Ethiopian woman, who represents the church which is drawn out from among the Gentiles.

The Synagogue represented by Miriam and the priesthood represented by Aaron, opposed having their authority taken away and given to other people. It was Origen's view that Moses' connubial bond with the Ethiopian woman caused Moses to receive his indorsement from Yahweh. Moses had never received such high accolades nor commendations for all of his exploits and accomplishments from God as he received when he married the Ethiopian woman. It is believed that this trend of thinking was the result of the harmony that prevailed in the early church in Alexandria where Romans, Greeks, Jewish Christians, Ethiopians, Arabs and Indians shared a common relationship.

Origen stated that an individual's soul may be black with sins but becomes beautiful through the act of repentance. The one who says "I am black and beautiful" does not retain that blackness but enables the daughters of Jerusalem to say, "Who is this that comes up having been made white?"

Origen suggested, according to Pope (1977: 310), that the blackness involved in this explanation is not the result of a natural condition but rather the result of circumstance or force because "the sun looked down on me."

> This shows, according to Origen, that she is not speaking of bodily blackness, because the sun tans or blackens when it looks *at*, and not when it looks down *on*. Origen stated that "The Sun of Justice did not look (directly) at the Gentile Church, but looked askance (Ruffinus makes a play on *despicere* and *adspicere*). The blackness then for which she is reproached resulted from the sun having looked at her askance because of her unbelief and disobedience. But when he repents and he looks at her directly, then her light will be restored and her blackness completely banished.

Pope correctly notes, "Thus by dint of some fancy exegetical footwork, Origen outdid himself again and undermined his own positive approach to the theology of negritude."

Oswald Neuschotz de Jassy in 1914, (cited by Pope 1977: 311) declared that the "Black Beauty of the Canticle" is none other than the Egyptian goddess Isis and that the Song of Solomon is a lament prompted by the death of the Egyptian god Osiris. The influence of the Isis cult on Christianity has long been recognized. King (1887, 173, cited by Pope 1977: 312), noted,

> The Black Virgins so highly venerated in certain French Cathedrals during the long night of the Middle Ages, proved when at last examined by antiquarian eyes to be the basalt statues of the Egyptian goddess, which having merely changed the name, continued to receive more than pristine adoration. Her devotees carried into the new priesthood the ancient badges of their profession; "the obligation to celibacy, the tonsure, the bell and the surplice.

Wittekindt (1926, cited by Pope 1977: 312) suggested that the black and burnt one was the same as Ishtar, a lunar goddess. The blackness was the result of the waning moon which, when it disappears, becomes dark and is married to the sun. Her reappearing indicates that she is pregnant and getting larger. Wittekindt lists many other black goddesses for our consideration, such as:

> the Black Dementer, the Many Breasted Artemis of Ephesus, the Black Aphrodite of Corinth, the Black Representations of the Virgin Mary (madonna nera), the Black Balti (=Ishtar) in Harran, and the various black stones representing goddesses, including the Black Stone of the Ka'ba-t at Mecca.

Durand-Lefebvre (1937, cited by Pope [1977: 313]) made a special investigation of black madonnas found in churches and monasteries in Europe. Among the many hypotheses that contributed to their blackness are the following:

1. Discoloration in the material, the result of natural causes.
2. The selection "of the ethnic type" as a model.
3. Oriental origin of a model derived from Asia.
4. Symbolic sense based on passages from the Canticles used in the office of the Virgin.
5. Survival of ancient cults.

Durand-Lefebvre admitted that in some situations the coloration of the effigies may have been caused by smoke or fire or made of black wood or stone such as ebony or basalt, chosen because of easy access or because of some quality other than its blackness. The use of black paint strongly suggests that the nigritude was not a matter of accident, but an intrinsic and necessary attribute of the Virgin.[33]

The grotto of Demeter became a Christian shrine dedicated to Panagia and a fecund black goddess who was succeeded by the Virgin Mary. Similarly, black images of the goddess Isis were acceptable in many places.

> Because the transition from paganism for which the name of Isis stood was a stealthy and insensibly prolonged blending rather than a sudden disruption, statues like the one in Paris might stay inside Christian churches without arousing comment. Images of Isis could become "black Madonnas" (R.E. Witt, 1971–274).

From a Jewish text of the eleventh century A. D., the *Midrash Leqah Tob of Tobiah Ben Eliezer*, comes a commentary on Numbers 21:29 ("Woe to you O Moab! You are undone, O people of Chemosh") which speaks of Chemosh being worshipped as a Black Goddess:

> This is Chemosh, the Abomination which is in the desert (*midbar*). It is black stone, its form like that of a black woman. It was in the midst of the high place (bamah) and Moab and her environs used to go to it to worship her. Thus it says (Judg 11:24): "Will you not possess what Chemosh your god gives you to possess?" That is, in the tongue of Ishmael (i.e. Arabic), Makkah (i.e. Medda), ...[34]

Pope notes that Chemosh was assumed to have been a male deity, but the compound of Ashtar-Chemosh of the Mesha Stela provokes a question as to whether or not the compound word represent male or female deity. He notes:

> Although scant weight may be attached to a medieval midrash which identifies Chemosh as a black goddess and confuses Moab and Mecca, still the tradition is provocative and highly interesting when viewed in the context of the Song of Songs 1:5 and related to other black goddesses attested with greater certainty.[35]

One can only conjecture if Pope's strong case for "black and beautiful" was instrumental in the shift in the New Revised Standard Version, which has "I am black and beautiful," whereas the Revised Standard Version had "I am very dark, but comely."

However, there is another apparent negative expression concerning blackness in 1:6 which reads, "Do not gaze at me because I am dark, because the sun has gazed on me." Pope (1977: 321) renders this "Stare not at me that I am swart," hoping to make the reading non-committal. If the Shulammite woman was proud of being a black beauty, it is difficult to understand why she commands no one to look at her.

Dahood (1966: 302) translated the verse, "Do not envy me in that I am black." Pope disagreed, noting, "The blackness is striking and beautiful, but not necessarily enviable."

McDaniel (1992) has offered the following suggestion. In Hebrew the negative particle *'al* when followed by an imperfect or jussive (i.e., a shortened imperfect) form of the verb, indicates generally a negative imperative, as is the case in 1:6, *'al tirah* "look you not." However, it has long been recognized by Gordon (1965: 76–77) that the exact same form can be taken as an asservative (emphatic positive) command.[36] This *positive* force of a negative particle is in Gordon's opinion probably due to a common linguistic phenomenon of using a negative question to imply a positive fact: "is it not so" = "it is so."

In light of this linguistic feature in Ugaritic, McDaniel would translate the *'al tirah* in 1:6 as "take a good look at me!" With all due modesty the black and beautiful Shulammite woman was calling attention to herself. Her siblings were—as might be expected—more interested in how much work they could get out of her (1:6b) than being appreciative of her beauty. She had spent enough time in the vineyard of unappreciative brothers; she longed to be in the pasture with her adoring beloved.

Perhaps the next translation to be published will draw on the suggestions of Pope and McDaniel so that the Song of Solomon 1:5 will read: "I am black and beautiful, O daughters of Jerusalem, like the tents of Kedar, like the curtains of Solomon. Take a good look at me because I am dark, because the sun has gazed on me."

In light of the Greek myth which spoke of black Africans becoming scorched by the sun-chariot when the young god lost control of the sun and it went off course swooping close to earth over the lands south of the Mediterranean, we cannot be certain that the "sun-tanned" black beauty was a well tanned Caucasian. In McDaniel's opinion, Dahood (1964: 406) is probably correct in taking the unusual verb here to mean "make black as pitch." Pope correctly noted (1977: 322), "This [suggestion of Dahood] would *intensify* [italics mine] the very blackness which many critics have sought to mitigate."

THE TRIBE OF DAN
AND THE FALASHAS OF ETHIOPIA

Although the Falashas are not mentioned in the biblical text, they deserve attention in this study of Blacks in the Bible. According to tradition the Falashas are related to the tribe of Dan and can, therefore, be called "Black Israelites" or "Black Hebrews." However, since they are also thought to be related to Solomon, they can be called "Black Judeans" or "Black Jews."

The following is the story that places Dan in Ethiopia and relates the Danites and the Falashas. According to a legend cited by Ginzberg (1938: 182), Jeroboam, the ruler of the northern kingdom of Israel, desired to terminate the religious dependency northern Israel had with the southern kingdom of Judah and temple of Jerusalem. It was his desire to bring about a war with the southern kingdom. But, according to the legend, "the people of the northern kingdom refused to enter into hostility with their brethren and with the ruler of their brethren, who was a descendant of David, the ruler of the earlier United Kingdom."

In his craftiness, Jeroboam approached the elders of the northern Israel, to bring them into play. They suggested that he employ the services of the Danites who were the most expert and decisive warriors in Israel.[37] The Danites refused Jereboam's request on the basis that they too would never shed the blood of their kinsman. As a result, a revolution against Jeroboam was brewing among the members of the tribe of Dan. However, it was not consummated because the word of Yahweh encouraged the Danites, instead, to leave Israel.

In the legend, many alternatives came to the mind of the Danites rather than journeying to Egypt; but they finally decided to journey through Egypt to Ethiopia. Because of the reputation of the Danites, the Egyptian warriors were terrorized and stationed their best warriors on the roads that would be traversed by the Danites. When the Danites arrived in Ethiopia they slew part of the citizenry and demanded tribute from those who survived.

41

According to Wurmbrand (1971: 1143–1154) the name Falashas
was attached to these non-indigenous Ethiopians by the natives of
Ethiopia with whom they lived. It means "exiled" or "immigrants."[38] These "immigrants" were a tribe of dark skinned
"Jews" in Abyssinia (Ethiopia). As reported by Schmerler (1941:
234) they refer to themselves as *Beta-Israel* ("the House of Israel"),
and with pride trace their genealogy from the stock of Abraham,
Isaac and Jacob. The Falashas as "Beta Israel" or, more popularly
now, "Black Jews" were considered to be in direct descent from the
patriarch Abraham, the first "Hebrew."

According to their own tradition, as reported by Schmerler (1941:
234), the Falashas traced their origin back to the retinue who
journeyed with Prince Menelik, the son of Solomon and the Queen
of Sheba, when he went home to Ethiopia.

Scientific theories suggest that the Falashas are of Hamitic (Cush-
itic) origin and are a part of the Agau tribes which were a part of the
Ethiopian population before the arrival of Semitic tribes from
southern Arabia. Ethiopian historical records indicate that the
religion of Judaism was wide spread before changing to the Christian
faith during the Axumite Kingdom in the fourth century B.C. The
Falashas are monotheistic and until recent times considered themselves to be the only Israelites remaining in the world. Legend aside,
much controversy has surrounded their origin.

Schmerler (1941: 234) cited Joseph Halevy, who traveled in
Abyssinia in 1868, as saying:

> that the Falashas come from the Judaizing Himyarites captured in Ethiopia by King
> Caleb: these Himyarites took refuge in the mountains beyond the Takazze and
> converted a part of the Agaus (the Aborigines of Abyssinia) the Falashatite being
> produced by intermarriage.

Schmerler, then noted:

> Nahoum, the former grand Rabbi of Turkey, considers them to be natives of the
> country, converted to Judaism by a group of Egyptian Jewish emissaries in the
> second or third century. Jacques Failovitch [1905] suggests that the light black color
> of their skins and their finely cut, regular features characterize them as a non-
> African race. He believes that they were originally Jewish immigrants possibly from
> upper Egypt, descendants of those Jews who settled in Egypt after the first exile.

It is believed that the Falashas who remained faithful to their teaching of Judaism (which was "a pure Mosaism based upon the Ethiopic version of the Pentateuch," but with a knowledge of the Apocrypha, though no knowledge of Hebrew) were persecuted and forcefully pushed from the coastal region into the mountains in the north around Lake Tana. There they concentrated their number and enjoyed political independence under their own leaders.

The Jewish captives whom the *Negus* Kalb returned following his military campaign in 525 B. C. (*negus* is Amharic for "king" and the title of the sovereign of Ethiopia) against Joseph Dhu Nuwas, King of Himyar, congregated in the general region of Semyen and added to the population which adhered to the Jewish religion. This combined group is known as the Falashas.

The Falashas played an active part in the revolution of the Agau tribes against the Axum monarchy in the tenth century. In 947 A. D., we learn from tradition, a queen named Judith (or Esther) led rebel tribes in deposing the *negus* and displayed their anger against Christian churches, the Christians and their monasteries. Queen Judith forced from the Ethiopian throne the ruler who was in the dynastic line of Solomon and Sheba.

The Falashas ruled the nation of Ethiopia for forty years. In the year of 1270, a descendant from the Axum dynasty, with the help of the Christian church, returned to the throne and brought an end to the independence of the Falashas. He could not depend upon the Falasha loyalty in war against the muslim kingdoms situated on the southeastern border of Ethiopia. Two kings, Amda Siyon and Ishaq, were successful in defeating the Falashas. The existence of a number of churches in Wogara and Dembea, areas that were inhabited by the Falashas, is evidence that they voluntarily converted to Christianity or were forced to do so.

In the succeeding years, from 1434 up to and including approximately 1634 A. D., the Falashas experienced many massacres in desperate efforts to convert them to the Christian church of Ethiopia. They were given promises that were broken and found themselves victims of intense massacres, even in the usurpation of their lands as well as being sold as common slaves.

Under every *negus*—from Zar'a Ya'kub to Baeba Maryam, Lebna Dengel, and Susenyos—the Falashas experienced bitter cruelty. Yet, despite tragic efforts to seemly exterminate this tribe which persistently and tenaciously adhered to their Jewish laws, rituals and feast, the Falashas remained faithful to their religious convictions.

Wurmbrand (1971: 1144–1154) noted that Jacques Failovitch, at the beginning of the twentieth century, helped to improve the condition of the Falashas. He intervened for them with *Negus* Menelik II (1889–1913). Failovitch was responsible for the formation of "pro-Falashas committees" which brought into existence mobile schools that went from village to village and gave to young Falashas training and instruction in various fields of learning. Many of the young Falashas were able to reside in boarding schools in Addis Ababa and some were even able to study in Europe as well as in Israel.

Because of this training some Falashas were able to secure government positions of significance. Wurmbrand (1971: 1150) also noted that at the time of the Italian Occupation (1936–1941), the Falashas demonstrated their loyalty to *Negus* Haile Selassie. When Ethiopia was liberated, the life of the Falashas reverted to the former trend and it was uncertain how they would be affected by modern improvements in Ethiopia under the new rulers. As Snowden (1970) noted, the late Haile Selassie, "the Lion of Judah," who mounted the throne of Ethiopia in 1930, was the last of the line of Solomon and Sheba, having died while under house arrest in 1957.

The Falashas rigidly practice the Jewish customs of cleanliness. They live in separate residences and in their villages isolate themselves from other inhabitants. Non-Jews are not permitted to enter their dwellings. Because they are so adamant with regard to cleanliness, they try to establish themselves in their settlements beside a river or a moving stream of water.

The Falashas, like all Ethiopians, believe in spirits (zar) which have the ability to control people. They also involve themselves in sorcery not for the purpose of doing injury to their neighbors, but rather to heal the sick, to comprehend the future, to discover the whereabouts of lost objects or animals, to control nature such as causing it to rain or to stop hail from falling. Their invocations draw upon magical prayers, charms, and employ strange names for angels, spirits and God. These prayers used to undo spells, offset the effects of the evil eye or disease caused by it. It is believed that those who were involved in pottery manufacturer made objects that elicited, provoked or enhanced the fertility rights of the Falashas believers.

The Falashas are conversant with the Apocrypha and other books of the Bible. Schmerler (1941: 234–235) provided a summary of the main religious customs of the Falashas. The major features of which follow in the next several paragraphs.

In every settlement where they are found there is a building called *Mesgid* ("the place of prayer") or *Beta Egziabeher* ("the house of God"). It is interesting to note, also, the diverse religious leadership among the Falashas. There are *menokossie, kahens* (which is related to the Hebrew *kohen* "priest"), *debteras*, Nazarites, priests and learned men. It is the *debtera* who instructs the children to understand the prayers of the sacred scriptures, the Pentateuch and the Book of Psalms, and the reading and writing of Amharic. The *debtera*, is also the assistant to the priest and has been a student of the sacred text but has not been ordained to the elevation of a priest. The priests wear a headdress while the other Falashas go bare headed. The *kahen* shares social interaction with other Falashas. He must marry but cannot remarry when the first wife dies. They are the ones to do the ritualistic slaying of the animals that are sacrificed. The Falashas practice the Mosaic ritual of frequent sacrifices.

The Falashas do not eat raw meat like other Ethiopians nor will they eat meat slaughtered by Christians. They recite blessings before and after they eat a meal. Because they are not conscious of Talmudic prohibitions of eating milk and meat together, they share these two items jointly on the Sabbath day. All biblical feasts, according the mosaic law, are celebrated according to the ceremonial regulations and guidelines with the exception Hanukah and Purim.

Circumcision among them is performed on the eighth day and should the eighth day fall on Saturday, it is moved up to Sunday. Girls are also circumcised, but this right is executed by the women.

The Falashas are monogamous and are opposed to mixed marriages. They live an exemplary life and as a result the Falashas are able to escape the ravages of venereal disease which is rampant in Ethiopia. They feel that they are "superior to their neighbors in hygiene, morals, physical well-being, and character." Because the women are emancipated, they work side-by-side with the men unaffected by the restrictions that are placed upon the females of their Abyssinian neighbors. A legal marriage requires only the presence of witnesses for the ceremony. Divorce is rare.

The classical and literary language of the books they read are written in Gheez, the language of Abyssinia. They are mainly engaged in agriculture pursuits and manual labor. However, many of them are skilled artisans engaged in pottery, spinning, weaving, basketry, blacksmiths and goldsmiths.

Many estimates are given to the number of Falashas that live in Ethiopia. A Scottish traveler in the 18th century by the name of James Bruce estimated that they numbered 100,000. Henry Stern, a missionary, estimated in the middle of the 19th century that there were a quarter million. Failovitch, in the early twentieth century, proposed the number of 50,000 but R. Hayyim Nahum estimated that it was only about 7,000 Falashas in the country. Wolf Leslau suggested that in 1949 there were about 15,000 or 20,000. In 1969 it was estimated that they may number 25,000 to 30,000. Their exact number was not certain.

The most dramatic change in the life of modern Falashas came in "Operation Solomon," when on May 24–25, 1991 about 14,500 Falashas were airlifted out of Ethiopia and flown to Israel. As reported in *Time* on June 3, 1991:

> The Israeli government took advantage of the confusion surrounding the resignation and departure of President Mengitsu Haile Manariam to launch a massive airlift to some 14,000 Ethiopian Jews who fearfully gathered near the Israeli Embassy. Using giant C-130 transport planes and seven 747 jets, the Israeli military removed the Jews, known as Falashas, in just 33 hours.[39]

EBED MELEK

In I Chronicles 28:1, the officials of Israel are divided into the following categories: "the officials (*sarîm* literally, 'princes') of the tribes, the officers (*sarîm*) of the divisions that served the king, those (*sarîm*) who command thousands of men, those (*sarîm*) that command hundreds of men, the stewards (*sarîm*) of the kings property, the kings cattle and his sons, along with all the *sarîsîm*, and all the mature well-trained warriors (*gibbôrîm*)." We now turn our attention to a man who was among the *sarîsîm* and had the courage to confront the *gibbôrîm* in the defense of Jeremiah. This is a character who deserves more attention than the nine lines he received in Bishop Dunstan's (1974: 137) study of Black men in the Old Testament or the twelve lines he receives in Bright's (1965) Anchor Bible commentary.

The Ethiopian Ebed Melek appears in Jeremiah 38:7–14 as a *saris* attached to the royal palace of King Zedekiah. The Hebrew word *saris* has two different meanings and may indicate a servant of high rank, as in II Kings 25:19) or low rank (as in I Kings 22:9. As de Vaux (1961:121) pointed out, it means an "officer" or a "courtier" when it is the loan word from Assyrian, *sha reshi* "one who is at the head," i.e. one "who goes before the king, one of the king's confidential advisors."

It can also have the meaning of a chamberlain for the woman's quarters, carrying the meaning of the Arabic *sarasa* "to be impotent," as noted in the Hebrew lexicons[40] which generally give the meaning "a castrated male." The term *saris* according to Rice appears some forty-five times in the Old Testament, and it is not always clear which meaning it should have—an "officer" of high or low rank or a "eunuch."

Among those called a *saris* were Potiphar, Pharaoh's "captain of the guard," Genesis 37:36, and Pharaoh's chief cup bearer and chief baker, Genesis 40:2 (NRSV "his two officers" for Hebrew *sarisayw*). The attendants of the king were divided into two classes, as seen in

I Samuel 8:15, which speaks of the king's *'abadîm* "servants" and his *sarîsîm* "officers" or "eunuchs." When Jerusalem fell the Israelite fighting men of war were commanded by *sarîs* (II Kings 25:19 and Jeremiah 52:25), which Gray (1970: 768) and Bright (1965: 365), respectively, translated "one officer" and "a certain official."

Consequently, a *sarîs* might be a person of high social, military, and political position and be very wealthy financially. As Rice (1975: 100) noted, Nathan-Melek, who resided in the vicinity of the temple in Jerusalem, was such a *sarîs* (II Kings 23:11). As will be seen, Ebed Melek probably had equal status in the kings court.

The second reference about Ebed Melek is in Jeremiah 39:16. Ebed Melek was a Cushite, and since his name can mean "servant/slave of the king" and since he could have been a eunuch, no one has challenged the equation here of Cush with Ethiopia. There has been no attempt to make Eded Melek a Midianite or a Kassite, as was the case with Moses' Cushite wife.

Racial stereotyping has played havoc with Ebed Melek's reputation. For some, like Lockyer (1958: 94) his being a Cushite meant that he was a heathen of non-Semitic origin, one of a despicable type, black in color. But as Adamo (1986: 204–205) pointed out:

> If [the eunuch] Ebed-melech is a practicing Israelite who worships Yahweh as suggested by the prophet Jeremiah's saying (Jer. 39:15–18) that he trusted in Yahweh, he could not have been a prince or in the congregation of the Israelite. [sic] Israelite law prohibits a eunuch from their congregation (Deut 23:1, Lev. 21:17–21).

As discussed above in dealing with Moses' Cushite wife, the term Cush is usually designated in the Septuagint and the Latin Vulgate by Ethiopian, "burned face," generally identified with the region in the Southern Nile River Valley beginning at the first cataract of the Nile (Aswan) and proceeding indefinitely to the South. Sometimes the term Nubian is used to designate the approximate area which dates from the time of the Roman Empire. It is the equivalent of the state of Sudan.

The Bible is silent as to where, when, or how Ebed Melek was introduced to Zedekiah, the last king of Judah. One can conjecture that his introduction to the Israelite court could have come from an alliance made earlier between the Sabean or the Shabeans (Ethiopians) and the Israelites during the time of Solomon. He could have been a mercenary soldier. For whatever reason, the term *sarîs* 'eunuch' does not bare the same connotation when applied to him as was the case with other males. Rather, *sarîs* "an overseer, an officer," or a *leader* in the administration of King Zedekiah seems more likely.

McDaniel (1992) suggested that Ebed Melek could well have been a recent descendent of the deposed Twenty-Fifth Dynasty that ruled Egypt from 716–663 B. C. When the Cushite dynasty came to its end at the hands of Essarhaddon, they were *deported* from Egypt. This can hardly mean they were sent back to Ethiopia where they could regroup and renew the conflict. Rather they were scattered through the Assyrian empire, which included the land of Israel and the kingdom of Judah.

The Twenty-Fifth Dynasty did not come to an end easily. Essarhaddon's own words tell of the power of his Cushite adversaries. In the Senjirili inscription he states:[41]

> From the town of Ishhupri as far as Memphis, his [Tirhakah's] royal residence, a distance of 15 days (march), I fought daily, without interruption, very bloody battles against Tirhakah (Tarqû), king of Egypt and Ethiopia, the one accursed by all the great gods. Five times I hit him with the point of (my) arrows (inflicting) wounds from which he should not recover, and then I led siege to Memphis, his royal residence, and conquered it in a half a day by means of mines, breaches and assault ladders; I destroyed (it), tore down (its walls) and burned it down. His "queen," the women of his palace, Ushanahuru, his "heir apparent," his other children, his possessions, horses, large and small cattle beyond counting, I carried away as booty to Assyria. All Ethiopians I deported from Egypt—leaving not even one to do homage (to me). Everywhere in Egypt I appointed new (local) kings, governors, officers (*šaknu*), harbor overseers, officials and administrative personnel.

Ebed Melek's roots could well have been among the displaced administrative personnel of the court of the defeated Tirhakah. Ebed Melek occupied a position of such significance that he was able to gain access to the king in matters of political and military importance. The scripture states that Ebed Melek was able to communicate directly his thoughts to the king, with no fear of reprimand or rebuke. Ebed Melek sought and found Zedekiah at the Benjamin gate, perhaps when he was overseeing preparations in anticipation of the return of the Babylonian forces. Moreover, the king listened to what he had to say and acted in accordance with his suggestions.

Whatever may have been his religious tradition, Ebed Melek believed that Jeremiah was an emissary of the God of Israel. News had come to him through conversation heard directly or indirectly that Jeremiah —the prophet who had been God's mouthpiece during the reign of Josiah, Jehoiakim, Jehoiachin, and Zedekiah—had been cast into a cistern on the property of Prince Malkiah. There, it was believed, he would either drown in the mud, starve because of no food, or suffocate for the lack of air. The ultimate objective was to make sure Jeremiah, who had begun his ministry forty years earlier, died.

Ebed Melek's plea pricked the king's conscience and he ordered Ebed Melek to take with him three or thirty men. The NRSV, like the RSV, has "three men," whereas the KJV has "thirty men." Bright (1965: 231) noted,

> *"Take with you three of these men here.* I.e., of those in attendance upon the king. Heb. reads 'thirty'; but that this is far more men than would have been needed, and is probably an error, as commentators agree.

But as McDaniel (1992) noted, the evidence for emendation is very slim. One manuscript in Kennicott's 1780 critical edition of the Hebrew Bible has the feminine singular *šlšh* instead of *šlš*, and one manuscript in the Greek (MS 449) has *trikonta tessara* "thirty-four," instead of "thirty." McDaniel suggested that emendation is not required. The *šalošîm* (consistently taken to be here the mistaken plural of *šaloš* "three") is, in McDaniel's opinion, more likely to be the Hittite loanword, *šalliš*, recognized by Cowley (1920: 327) more than seventy years ago (although Cowley did not connect this loanword with Ebed Melek). Cowley noted:

> The precise meaning of the title *šalîš* in the O. T. has been unsuccessfully discussed since the days of Origen. An obvious derivation from *šlš* would make it mean 'a third man' or 'one of the three', and it is accordingly rendered by the LXX as *tristatēs*. This has been explained by Origin, and most scholars since, as meaning 'the third man in a chariot'. . . But even if it were the fact that a chariot carried three men, of whom one was an officer, the explanation would be unsuitable to the passages in which the word occurs.

The Hittite *šalliš* in Cowley's words,

was borrowed by Hebrew at a time when the Hittites were still powerful in Syria. In that case it has nothing to do with 'three', but means an important official in close attendance on the king.

This meaning, as Cowley noted, makes sense in Exodus 14: 7 ("all the cavalry [chariots] of the Egyptians and *šališîm* over it all"); Exodus 15:4 ("the best of his *šališîm*"); I Kings 9:22 ("his *šališîm* and the officers of his cavalry"); II Kings 7:2 ("the *šališ* of the king, on whose hand he had leaned); II Kings 9:25 ("and he [Jehu] said to Bidkar his *šališ*"); II Kings 10:25 ("and Jehu said to the guard and the *šališîm*"); and II kings 25:25 ("and Pekah his *šališ* conspired against him").[42] It also makes sense in Jeremiah 38:7 where Ebed Melek, the *sarîs,* was entrusted with the *šališîm* of King Zedekiah, probably the king's personal military security unit.

Ebed Melek not only interceded on Jeremiah's behalf but was also instrumental in having him released from the cistern, his potential place of death. Because he was knowledgeable as to the supplies, where they were, what they were and their condition, he went to the storeroom directly and secured the material needed on this rescue mission. As a *sarîs* he had obvious respect from the military force, the *šališîm* that accompanied him. There is no suggestion of any question regarding his authority by the *šališîm* who went with him or the military unit guarding Jeremiah, who received him. Instructing Jeremiah to place the rags between his armpits and the ropes Ebed Melek and his men rescued Jeremiah from the muck and mire of the cistern, from the dank and foul air of imprisonment and escorted him to the court of the guard where he remained until the fall of Jerusalem in 587 B. C.

The question can be raised, "were there actually "thirty" *šališîm* involved in this military assignment?" (with the original Hebrew having been *šalošîm šališîm* "thirty security-men," with the loss of one *šlšym* of the original wording). If so, this number would have discouraged any interference from any hostile military contingent.

As Calkins (1930: 298) commented, from historical obscurity to the immortal recognition and praise, this otherwise Black man rose to receive wide applause and praise. The second time Ebed Melek is mentioned in Jeremiah is in 39:16 – 18, where the word of Yahweh guaranteed his life and personal safety:

> I will rescue you on that day . . . you will not be handed over to the men of whom you are afraid . . . I will surely save you. You will not fall by the sword, but will come out of it alive, because you have trusted in me.

Thus a non-Semitic, non-Israelite, non-Judean, one who was not identified with the 'chosen' covenant people experienced a promise from God which was made to only one other person, namely Baruch, who in Jeremiah 45:5 was also promised to "have his life as a prize of war." As Ginzberg noted (1925: 96, 165) Ebed Melek and Baruch were in Jewish tradition among the select ten to twelve persons who were translated to heaven without passing *through* death. The promise of having one's "life as a prize of war" was taken to mean that neither Ebed Melek or Baruch would die. They share the glory of Enoch who "walked with God and was not."

Ebed Melek was not only a faithful servant of Zedekiah, but he was a sincere servant of the God of Israel. He lived up to the meaning of his name Ebed ("the servant of") Melek ("the king"). He was the servant (*ebed*) of the earthly king, and, at the same time, servant (*ebed*) of the heavenly King, Yahweh, the God of Israel. His faithfulness to both God and king led him to risk his own life to save the life of a prophet of God. He was rewarded for his faithfulness by having his life preserved by the God of all life. His life is a testimony to the fact that God is no respecter of persons and that "He will keep in perfect peace those whose minds are stayed on Him," be they Cushite or Israelite.

SIMON OF CYRENE

Nothing in Mark or Luke pointedly states or even suggests that Simon Cyrene was an Ethiopian or a Black. Only a syllogism based upon post-biblical stereotyping could make Simon a Black (other than the assumption that all the biblical characters were Black); namely, Simon was from Africa. Simon was pressed into service by the Romans, therefore Simon must have been Black.

Mark 15:21: reads "And they compelled one Simon a Cyrenian, who passed by, coming out of the country, the father of Alexander and Rufus, to bear his cross." Luke 23:26 reads "As they led him away, they laid hold of one Simon, a Cyrenian, coming out of the country, and on him they laid the cross, that he may bear it after Jesus." Matthew 27:32 noted simply, "As they were marching out, they came upon a man of Cyrene, Simon by name; this man they compelled to carry his cross."

Cyrene, *Kurenaios* in the Greek, was one of the North African cities located on the south Mediterranean coast. A large Jewish colony resided in this city at this time under the control of the Romans.

Mann (1986: 645) challenged other scholars, who wrote concerning Mark 15:21–32, that Simon's ethnic identification is not clear from the scriptural account. However, secular history gives unquestioned evidence that Cyrene was a White settlement in Africa, with a large Jewish population. It is, therefore, most probable that Simon of Cyrene, although identified with the *African* city of Cyrene, was a White and possibly a Jew. The fact alone that he was ordered to bear the cross does not justify the conclusion that he had to have been a Black.

At this period in history those who were relegated to the position of contempt in the eyes of the Roman soldiers were white skin and red hair folks of Thrace. They had been vanquished, subdued and subjected by the Roman military. The citizenry of this Thrace would at this time have been considered as the underclass.

It has been suggested by most commentators that Simon, given his Hebrew name, was a diaspora Jew. But this is somewhat problematic, since putting even a diaspora Jew in such a subservient position could have ignited the already volatile conditions in Jerusalem. It is just as likely that a *Gentile* of Cyrene—whose children had the common Greek name Alexander and the Latin name Rufus "Red-Head"—was called upon to bear the cross for the weakened prisoner. This need not have been a Black, for Blacks were regarded as persons with stature and importance, though red-headed Thracians were not.

Evans (1980: 22) noted:

> Furthermore, the Europeans, like the peoples of the Near East, engaged in the stereotyping of slaves. But beyond the "sambo" perception [that slaves had a predilection for lying, laziness, theft, drunkenness and lewdness], which all shared, the stereotypes that emerged in the two regions were different. In Europe for a time, Scythians were regarded as a slavish people. The Thrace became an important source of the supply for the slave trade and Thracian characteristics, such as red hair, came to be regarded as slave characteristics. An actor on the Roman stage wore a red wig as a signal to the audience that he was playing the role of a slave. The *Thracian name, "Rufus," came to be regarded as a typical slave name regardless of the slave's nationality."* (italics mine)[43]

McDaniel (1992) commented, "if Simon of Cyrene had red hair like that of his son Rufus, a name which means "Red Head," he would have been the most natural choice by a Roman looking for someone to do a slave's chore.

The Greek text lends no clue as to whether this man was a Jew or a Gentile. He could have been a (red hair) Gentile proselyte to Judaism. In Acts 2:11, Luke stated that those who come from "around Cyrene" were Jews or proselytes. Thus, Simon could have been a Passover pilgrim journeying to Jerusalem to celebrate the religious festivities.

According to Kee (1962: 549), "Simon of Cyrene" has been equated with "Simon called Niger," mentioned in Acts 13:1. "Niger" has been taken to be a Latin loanword meaning "black." Consequently, there was the syllogism: "Simon of Cyrene = Simon called Niger; therefore Simon of Cyrene was a Black." However, McDaniel (1992) noted that "Niger," rather than being a Latin loanword, may well be the Semitic word *nagar* attested in Hebrew, Syriac, Arabic, Akkadian, and Ugaritic meaning "a carpenter" with the intensive form of the verb in Hebrew, *niggēr*, meaning "to do carpenter's work."[44]

According to Mann it was the customary practice for the condemned criminal to carry the *patibulum*, just the cross beam of the cross, on his shoulders. The vertical shaft of the cross would already have been set up. Simon of Cyrene, therefore, following Jesus, carried this part of the cross of Jesus from a gate in Jerusalem along the winding road known as the Via Dolorosa to the crown of the hill known as Golgotha.

We can well assume that Jesus was weakened by the ordeal of being flogged thirty-nine times. (Tradition tells us that it was not uncommon for victims to die from the severity of this type of punishment.) According to Irenaeus (*Adveresus Haereses* 1.24.4) the Gnostics used this item in tradition to declare that it was not Jesus who died but Simon.

Mark is the only gospel that reveals to us that Simon was the father of Alexander and Rufus. We can assume that either Mark knew them personally or the source from which Mark obtained his information knew the sons of Simon. Paul, in Romans 16:13, acknowledged him as a person he knew. Church tradition reveals that his two sons were saved, however, we do not know if Simon received the Lord Jesus Christ as his personal Savior or not.

PHILIP AND THE ETHIOPIAN EUNUCH

Acts 8:26–39 provides a New Testament text for an African connection in the early church. This story starts with Philip, one of the seven chosen by the congregation to administer to the needs of the widows, who was directed to go from Jerusalem to Gaza shortly after he arrived in Jerusalem from Samaria. According to Munck (1967: 78), the road that Philip used led to the coastal plain along the Mediterranean Sea, the main thoroughfare traversed by caravans going south to Egypt.

The Greek text uses here the word *erēmos* "desolate, lonely, solitary," without being clear if it was the road or town which was deserted. It would be surprising to find this caravan road deserted. Therefore, Munk translated "this is the desert road," even though the road was along the coastal plain. But Munck noted that the town of Gaza, itself, may have been in ruins since it was destroyed by Alexander the Great.

Philip does not get into the city of Gaza but somewhere on that caravan highway either before the city of Gaza is reached or beyond the city itself, Philip sees this Ethiopian in his chariot on the way to Ethiopia.

Munck suggest that the Ethiopians were Nubians living between Aswan and Khartoum in upper Egypt and the Sudan; they were not as later then assumed, identical with the Abyssinians. The Ethiopian was called a *eunochos* "a eunuch" and recognized as a personage of great authority under the reign of Candace who is queen of the Ethiopians. He is in charge of all of her treasure and came to Jerusalem to worship Yahweh.

As discussed above in the study of Ebed Melek, the title eunuch does not necessarily mean a castrated male who cared for the harem. As its Akkadian equivalent, *ša reši* "one who is the head," indicates, a "eunuch" could be an important royal official.

Candace, according to Munck, was not the personal name of a particular queen or princess but a title used for the sovereign queen of Ethiopia at this point in time in their period of history—like

56

"Pharaoh" which was a title of authority and power over a large number of subjects.

Foster (1985) in a note in the New International Version of the Bible stated that the traditional title of Queen Mother who was responsible for performing the secular duties of the reigning King is couched in the title Candace. It was believed that the reigning King was too sacred a personage to be involved in secular activities.

The journey of this Ethiopian who was returning from a pilgrimage in Jerusalem, indicates that he was a believer or a Gentile proselyte and worshipper of Yahweh, the God of the Israel.

The text indicates that Philip was close enough to the Ethiopian's chariot that he heard the man reading the words from the prophesy of Isaiah. (According to Foster, it was a customary practice for persons reading Hebrew to read out loud that both their ears and mouth might become acquainted with the Hebrew sounds.) Philip broke in upon the eunuch's study of the passage, commonly referred to as the "suffering servant" text, by asking him the question, "Do you understand what you are reading?"[45] The eunuch answered the question by asking another question "how can I unless someone explains it to me?" Philip was invited to mount the chariot, sit with him and clarify for him the one about whom this scripture was referring.

Jesus had commissioned His disciples in the Matthew 28:19 first to teach believers then baptize them. This is what Philip did with the eunuch. The text states "that Philip began with the very passage of scripture that the eunuch had been reading but could not understand and told the eunuch about the way of salvation accomplished through Jesus Christ." Nothing we read tells us that Philip suggested baptism when the eunuch believed that Jesus Christ was the Son of God.

Apparently, the study of the Bible continued while the Ethiopian and his entourage were still moving along the coastal caravan route. As they journeyed along this road, they came to some water at an unspecified place. Foster suggested that the baptismal could have taken place in a brook located in the valley Elah (where David crossed to meet Goliath), or the Wadi-el-Hasi (just north of Gaza), or water from a spring or one of the many pools in the area.

The eunuch then said to Philip "look, here is water why shouldn't I be baptized"? In the neutral text, according to Munck, the baptism took place on the initiative of Philip, without any assistance from the

Ethiopian. The Western text has added verse 37 reading: "and Philip
said to him, 'if you believe with all your heart thou may.' And he
answered and said, 'I believe that Jesus Christ is the Son of God.'"
It would appear that the eunuch who was asking for baptism had also
made a confession of his faith. The eunuch gave orders to stop the
chariot and then Philip and the eunuch went down into the water and
Philip baptized him. When they came out of the water the spirit of
the Lord suddenly took Philip away and the eunuch did not see him
again but went on his way rejoicing to the land of Ethiopia.[46]

Tradition tells us that this eunuch became the first missionary
preacher to the Ethiopians witnessing his own conversion and
baptism to the people with whom he ministered and was responsible
for not only leading many Ethiopians to Christ but he is also
responsible for establishing the first Christian church in that country.

PART TWO

SERMON SUGGESTIONS
ON BLACKS IN THE BIBLE

INTRODUCTION:
NEVER FORGET WHO YOU ARE
AND TO WHOM YOU BELONG

The tragedy of many individuals who have been instrumental in leading people from the bondage of human weaknesses (their unawareness of God) is that they themselves can be caught in the same situation from which they have liberated others. We can become cocky with regard to our own importance and we can become intoxicated with the applause and praise of the emancipated souls and find ourselves playing into the hand of the arch enemy of humanity – self-righteousness.

Initially, we were selected, prepared, and empowered by God himself. It was not the wisdom nor the knowledge that came from our human understanding. It was not our words nor the convicting message that challenged the victims of enslavement nor was it our omnipotence nor might that prevailed to bring victory over their darkness. Behind the scenes, invisible to the human eye and beyond the range of human intelligence the omnipotence of God fractured and subdued the host of sin, that ultimately gave freedom to the enslaved.

It is God who has called us from the darkness of our own frustration into the glorious enlistment in His cause. It is He who has used us to sound the clarion note of victory. He could have done the complete job all by Himself. We are frail, incompetent and limited at our best but empowered by His spirit "we are more than conquerors through Him that loves us." Rephrasing Henley's poem "Invictus"

> It matters now how straight the gate;
> How charged with punishments the scroll.
> God is the captain of my fate.
> God is the master of my soul.

MIRIAM: A STUDY IN CONTRAST
Numbers 12:1

It is always disconcerting for us to see people in a different personal frame of mind other than what we are accustomed to seeing them. It is very difficult for us to accept change and somehow we fail to recognize that human emotions ebb and flow depending upon the motivating circumstances. Whatever we are accustomed to seeing a person do, to hearing what a persons says, or seeing how they act, is locked in our consciousness. We tend to think that he/she always will be and do and say the same thing as long as their life shall last. We are discernably shocked, upset, and disconcerted when human nature does not conform to our preset pattern of its activity.

Miriam, the eldest and only sister of Moses, was very stable and seemly emotionally secure. Her brothers were the recipients of her support and loyalty, especially the baby brother, Moses. Obedient to her mothers mandate, we find her watching, from a distance, her youngest brother floating in a reed bassinet on the Red Sea—watching lest any danger should challenge his life. When Pharaohs daughter with a retinue of attendants approaches the waters, Miriam is alert and ready to do whatever she can and as best she can in the interest of Moses. And when the little bassinet is emptied of its contents, and the baby Moses is brought to this personage of distinction, Miriam is prompted to intercede. This is her brother. "Do you want an Egyptian woman to nurse the baby," she inquires? Miriam is protective, concerned, and supportive of the welfare of little Moses.

The infant Moses has now matured into a Hebrew of commanding personality and poise. Tradition suggests that the oracles of the sacred Egyptian gods have declared him to be gifted with unusual skills and abilities. The Ethiopians, southern neighbors of Egypt, have delighted themselves in plundering and running as marauders over the land of Egypt killing and ravaging all in their path. Because they meet with little resistance their appetite to consume the whole of Egypt is wetted. Somehow the prophesy concerning Moses is brought to the attention of the Pharaoh. Moses' foster mother is ordered by her father (brother) to present Moses as a Commander for the

Egyptian forces. Despite the schemes and intrigues of some of the members of the royal family to terminate the life of Moses, his god-given knowledge enables him to lead the Egyptians under his command to victory after victory.

Watching the military skill and expertise of Moses, the daughter of the Ethiopian king, Tharbis, falls in love with Moses. She proposes a contract with him which he accepts provided that she fulfills her part of the agreement. The agreement was that she would commit the city into his hands and afterward he would take her for his wife. On the strength of this fulfilled agreement Moses married this Egyptian princess. This marriage of Moses to the Egyptian woman fractured the relationship between Moses and his sister Miriam giving rise to the first instance of racial prejudice in the scriptures.

Racial prejudice thrives on blind hatred and ignorance. It discards logical, factual information and is void of compassion and justice. Related and attended circumstances are negated. Background and contemporary history is canceled and obliterated.

This god-fearing woman exuberant in praise to Yahweh becomes a person to challenge even the wisdom of God. This loyal supportive sister now destroys in the flame of hate the sibling cord that bound her to her brother. This model of emotional exuberance extolling the omnipotence of God, now becomes a burned out ember of cynical criticism of God. Miriam has changed. This is a radical contrast to the personality that she once had. She not only has incited her personal feeling of resentment towards her brother Moses but she also provokes resentment in the mind and spirit of her brother Aaron. To add further insult to injury, she even challenges God's authority, wisdom, and power. Miriam is a study in contrasts.

The scene now changes and many years later we see a different Miriam. Assembled on the east bank of the Red Sea, in full view of this spectacular phenomena that has occurred before this motley host of a mixed multitude—animals and people, young and old, Jew and Gentile, a multi national mixture of people, Miriam breaks out in praise and exaltation to God for what He has done. The words, the rhythm, the music become contagious to the ears of the women in this aggregate assemblage and they all join in glorifying and mag-nifying God. Miriam did not accept what had transpired when the waters clapped their hands together and the armies of Pharaoh were drowned as a natural phenomenon.

She did not look upon this fantastic experience as the intervention of luck, nor as the visitation of the wrath of the gods of Egypt. Her mind, her spirit, her very being, recognized that God Himself had intervened in behalf of the children of Israel. She acknowledged and led other women to acknowledge that God was King of Kings and Lord of Lords.

Miriam moves from a loyal disciplined child, to a hostile woman who challenges the omnipotent God, to a woman whose personal experience and observation makes her magnify the transcended creator and sustainer of all life.

TOUCH NOT MY ANOINTED
Numbers 12:8c

The overt display of indifference to right and wrong, the apparent resolute determination to ignore signs of impending danger, despite the innumerable messages that vividly portray the ultimate end of all personal and corporate injustice, humanity heedlessly ignores the warnings of ultimate retribution. Too often the object of human wrath is not the God who holds life in the hollow of his hand but rather the messenger whom God has selected to proclaim his absolute word.

The opposing force can assume the physical image of a nation, a corporate body, a city, a congregation, an industry, an elite club or an individual. Whatever and whoever challenges the individual who is the spokesman for the power, who represents the throne of authority, the challenger has tampered with a force greater than they. The writer of the Psalm 24 declares, "The earth is the Lord's, and the fullness thereof: the world, and they that dwell therein." Whether we wish to acknowledge it or not, as frail creatures of time we are hopelessly, helplessly, undeniably, dependent upon that spiritual force called God for our life, breath and existence. We really own nothing, or make nothing, for as the axiom of physics declares matter can neither be created nor destroyed. Human beings, at best, can modify or change the physical appearance of matter, but one can not make it.

When God selects, develops, and endows a human creature with the unique gift of declaring His word, a lot of God is involved in that creature. The spirit of God has wrestled with that man and won the contest. Defeated are the egocentric drives which would elevate the man over the spirit that endued him. Subdued is the will to glorify itself basking in its own intelligence to the will of the God who sends him. Hushed is the voice of reasoning that pre-analysis the effect of the message to the ears of the hearers. Consumed by the fire of God's spirit this new creation transformed by the holy awesome presence of that supernatural being called Yahweh declares, "Here I am," all of me, willing to do thy will, O God.

It is this human creation, anointed by the power of God, who is drawn into a covenanted relationship that ties him to the seven 'I Wills' found in Exodus 6:6 & 7 confirming the undeniable union of God with man. It is this awesome power that moves a man to stand fearlessly in the midst of impending death unafraid for his own life for he is protected by the unseen presence of heavens host. He can challenge and not be refuted, renounce and not cautiously select his words, demonstrate unbelievable acts and not be cut down in the midst of his demonstrations. He can smite a rock in the hot arid heat of the desert and cool, clear, water gushes forth from the rock; he engages in intimate conversation with God for forty days and displays no physical body defects for this interval of time without physical sustenance. This man displays evidence of being anointed by God.

There are people who can see these unusual manifestations of supernatural endowment upon select individuals whom God has chosen who are either stricken with blindness of disbelief, or rational insensitivity, who disregard what other people respect. Miriam at this time is a classic example of one who ignored what other people feared. She knew of Moses' supernatural endowment. She permitted her eyes to be covered by the sin of prejudice and thus she was blind to the discernment that Moses was selected and anointed by God as His special servant.

What other reason can we find for her hostility against this man who had championed the cause of God's people jeopardizing His life? What cause could whip her emotions into the frenzy that would challenge the abilities of this noble leader? What could erase from her mind her previous loyalties and recognition of the importance of the male members of the Hebrew family? What could so incite her that she in turn could prick and inflame the docile nature of her brother Aaron that he might recoil in resentment against his brother Moses? What was it that drove her, a frail creature of the dust, whose breath was in the hands of El-Shadi, to challenge the omniscience and omnipotence of God?

God, who hears everything, heard Miriam's criticism of Him and His anointed vessel, Moses. In judgmental anger He responded to her derogatory criticism of His mouthpiece, Moses and his marriage to the Ethiopian woman, Tharbis. Miriam was stricken with leprosy, a disease that made her unclean and isolated her from the social interaction of the children of Israel until she was clean of the disease.

My grandmother had a saying that comes to mind, "God does not like ugly and He is not stuck on beauty." We need to be extremely careful in what we say, in what we do, and even how we act in our position to those who are God's anointed vessels who represent Him in a world of sin.

UNEQUALLY YOKED
Exodus 4:25
II Corinthians 6:14

The term yoke takes us out of the urban setting of life and leads us to the early rural times where animals where employed to aid in the plowing and the sowing and the reaping and in the harvesting of crops from the field. Yoking involved two animals, usually with equal strength, equal height, the same breed who would pull either the plow, the farm machinery or the wagon loaded with the produce from the field. They worked together from early morning to noon when there was a secession from the work of the early day and returned for the second half of the days labors in the field.

The term yoke is also applied to marriage that involves a man and a woman who together share the responsibilities of husband and wife and parenting as long as they live. Together they meet with adversities and problems, share their joys and sorrows, and share each others life until their day on earth is over. To make the responsibilities easier to manage or tolerate, they should be supportive of each other so that each of them might have a less difficult time doing their part to make their joint responsibilities easier to bear.

Just as in the case when two animals are mismatched under the same yoke, the work is more difficult for the bigger one or for the taller one, so it is in a relationship of mismatched husband and wife. The yoke that binds them should recognize the fact that they have some things in common. That appreciation for some common values, their regard for certain qualities and their recognition that certain principles must be respected by both of them make their togetherness in this pursuit of life less strained for each of them. When these things are not the case, then we are inviting marital disaster, social problems, and family difficulties into the relationship.

Moses was an Israelite and was steeped in the culture of that ethnic group. Zipporah was a Midianite, the second wife that Moses is known to have, and according to tradition was not aware of Moses' selection and intimate involvement with Yahweh, the God of the Israelite people. Their marital state, (the outcome of Moses' defending Zipporah and her sisters from verbal abuse and physical injury from male shepherds at the well), was more an expression of appreciation from Zipporah's father, Jethro. Although she bore two sons for Moses, Gershom and Eliezer, she still did not share the reverential fear for God as the Israelites or Moses did. In her sight, Moses was just another ordinary man, gentle, protective, and compassionate no more or less. There is a very strong suspicion that she did not possess those characteristics in her personal makeup to enable her to share with Moses in times of stress and strain that he had experienced in his life while leading the children of Israel from where they had been in servile slavery to the outer regions of the promised land. Perhaps she was not equipped with an appreciation of leadership qualities or characteristics. Perhaps she was just an ordinary non-interested Midianite woman whose limits of involvement in her husband's life were circumscribed by the duties of preparing him food, washing and preparing his clothes and bearing him children. She may very easily have been unable to read or to write the language of the Hebrews. It is quite possible that she was never exposed to the traditions, the history, or the rituals of the Hebrew law. Zipporah was indeed limited in the response, support, and understanding that she could lend to Moses in his times of need. It is no wonder that she became vehemently upset when she had to circumcise Gershom to save the life of Moses mortally stricken by God.

So often today professional men and their wives are estranged because they share so little educationally, so little socially, and so little intellectually with one another. Their involvement in their work, the need for continual upgrading of their skills, in seminars, or post graduate classes, restricts their interaction and quality time with their spouses. Recreational activities, periodic vacations, weekly get togethers with one's spouse can help to alleviate this professional loneliness. Because of Moses' ascended relationship with the supernatural being, Yahweh, his support and comfort could not come from a human source but of necessity had to be in spiritual communication with God.

DOES GOD HEAR A SINNER'S PRAYER?
Genesis 21:17

In the Gospel of Saint John, Chapter 9:31, the Pharisees hurl this statement at the man whom Jesus healed of his blindness. Said they, "We know that God does not listen to sinners" (NIV). The King James version states "That God does not hear sinners pray." To be learned men in scripture, this statement reflects their ignorance of scripture truth.

We are "born in sin and shaped in iniquity," David says in Psalm 51 "and in sin did my mother conceive me." The only way that we can take advantage of the saving grace of God through Jesus Christ, is to call on the name of the Lord. The word declares "they that call upon the name of the Lord (Jesus) shall be saved." Romans 10:13. In the 14th chapter of Saint John, verse 6, Jesus says "No one comes to the Father except through me." Saint John 14 (NIV). So it would seem that if we are going to be emancipated from sin and made a son of God we must call on the name of the Lord Jesus Christ even though we are sinners, born in the filth of sin, shaped in the foulness of sin, but we must call on the name of Jesus to be delivered from the penalty of sin which is death.

In the story of Hagar and Ishmael, we are drawn to the condition of Hagar's son, Ishmael. There in the desert he is dying because the water has given out and there is no food to sustain his life. It is in the desert beneath the shade of a scrub bush when the lad calls on the name of God through tears. He has been exposed to the worship of Yahweh, the God of his father, Abraham. He is the son of a slave woman, Hagar. There is no record that he has experienced the Bar Mitzvah recognizing him as a man and a son of the chosen people. There is no indication in the Word that he has been accepted as a follower of the God of Israel. No record bears evidence that he is among "the chosen."

There in the desert sheltered only by a scrub bush, beneath the blazing rays of the tropic sun, dehydrated from the dissipation of the fluid in his body and no evidence of natural water to drink, this foreigner, this sinner calls on the name of the Lord. His mother, Hagar, weeps in frustration and anger and is helpless to fend off his approaching death. The young lad was too weak to speak to challenge the powers of life or death or to give argument to the circumstances that have brought him to where he is. He just weeps. His tears become more eloquent than words expressed from a soul in deepest need, touches the heart, reaches the ears of the Eternal Spirit of the Lord that broods over all creation. "The Lord heard the lad weep!"

Mercy, one of the attributes of the Lord, became personified and pled for the life of the boy in the holy court of eternal justice. This plea supplemented with the plea of mercy from Hagar caused divine justice, the final authority over life and death, to rescind the sentence of death for the boy and instead grant him a stay of execution. More over, the Lord God converses with the woman, Hagar, not to a Hebrew male and said to her, "What's the matter, Hagar? Don't be afraid; I have heard the boy crying as he lies there." He has called out to me. " Lift up the boy and take him by the hand for I will make of him a great nation."

If God does not hear a sinner's pray, why was His heart touched by the plea of mercy expressed in the tears of both the mother and the son? If God does not hear sinners pray, why did He speak to Hagar? She is a foreign slave. A female Ethiopian slave. She has no ethnic tie nor religious line or connection to me. This is the first Old Testament evidence that God spoke to a female in this way and manner. If God does not hear a sinners prayer, why did He make a promise, a covenanted promise to Hagar? How can any sinner be saved from the inevitable destination which is theirs if God does not hear them cry out for mercy to Him? God alone can dispense mercy or justice, He is the Lord God all by Himself.

MISSING: A CRY OF FORGIVENESS
Genesis 21:17c
Romans 10:13

I am appalled as I read from the scriptures of the life, the acts, the works of men of note who are portrayed on the canvas of the word of God, who refute God, injure their brother and fail to raise a cry for forgiveness for the damage they have done. Is there no word in their vocabulary to express regret for what they have said or the long term scourge imposed on others for what they have done? Is it a mark of their male ego that would be withered or crippled for all time and eternity that makes it impossible for them to acknowledge their fault? Is it vain pride that would reflect an element of weakness somewhere in the being of in their moral fibre? Is this a result of the perpetrator of sin who has removed this word from the sinners mind and made the creature more vulnerable to his attack? Whatever it was that was deleted from the lips of early man, the cry for forgiveness for the wrong he has done, or may have done, is very evident by its absence.

Adam, the first and only human father of the human family, violated the mandate of God that has stigmatized every member of the human family with the scourge of sin. He never said to God, "I am sorry, forgive me Lord." This superior creation that rivals the angels who are endowed with supernatural abilities, who is more human than divine, yet invested with an awesome reservoir of supernatural gifts and intelligence, can say no to the authority of God. This creation that has both breathed and molded into it the image and the likeness of God, can say no to the authority of God. This form of life that possesses a soul can say no to the authority of God and not be destroyed if he asks God to forgive him before the breath of God has left his body. He has never said for his disobedience, "Forgive me, I am sorry." He is a creature of the earth, endowed with superior intelligence, enhanced with the ability to communicate with the effulgence of the Father's glory, broke an agreement with God and never uttered the cry of forgiveness. This super creation of the intelligence of God, who challenges the creation of the angelic host, the distinct emissaries of the will of God, lost sight of the first command God gave to earthly human creatures, but he never uttered the cry, forgive me I am sorry for what I have done.

Noah was the man whom the scriptures declared to be right with God and blameless among the people of his day. He pleased God in the life he lived and the witness he bore before the flood, and was chosen to preach the word of God to the inhabitants of the city and its environs for more than 120 years. But this man let slip from his mind who he was and to whom he belonged. He and his family were directed by God to find shelter in an ark that God instructed him to build. While they were in the ark, rains came from the heavens on the earth for forty days and forty nights to remove from the earth every living creature that God had made. This prophet, preacher, builder, preserver of animal and human life came out of the ark and practiced a new profession, that of agriculture pursuit. He developed and made a grape arbor and from the grapes he extracted wine. The wine gained potency and the preacher/builder became intoxicated to the point that he passed out.

This was a new experience for him; in his former days he was discreet, modest and only zealous in declaring the word of God. Well doth the scripture say, "strong drink is raging and he that takes thereof is not wise." Strong drink caused him to lose his poise, the command of himself and the modest discretion of his person. Drink caused his head to spin, his thinking to become faulty, his intelligence disjointed and his speech irrational. The righteousness of God clothed Adam, covering his nakedness from the curious gaze of others and the non-appealing sight of himself. God clothed the man to give him respect in his own eyesight and to cover the result of his own experiment with untried nature. God clothed man with the skins of animals to verify the fact that without the shedding of blood there could be no remission of sin. God clothed man to introduce all humanity to the advent of His son who through the shedding of His blood reconciled all people into the family of God.

Noah extracted from the fruit of the ground a substance that caused him to expose his nakedness to the eyes of his son and which reduced Noah's respect of himself. He had been foolish enough to permit the lust of the flesh to depreciate him in the sight of his son and in an effort to redeem himself he rebuked his son when actually the rebuke should have been on him. His words came forth not as a mild censor to Ham but because of his clouded mind they took on the form of greater proportion and became a curse. This curse has been misunderstood, modified, augmented, twisted by others to become a scurrilous stigma on the progenitors of Ham. Noah, when he became sober, never reconsidered what he had said nor the harm he had done to his son. Throughout sacred history we have yet to see Noah expressing regret or a cry for forgiveness to Ham or to Ham's offspring.

TURNING OFF THE WRATH OF GOD
Numbers 12:13

In the book of I Chronicles 16:22, and Psalm 105:15, we find these words "Do not touch my anointed ones; do my prophets no harm."(NIV) Familiarity has a tendency to breed contempt for in the interaction of one person with another under varied conditions and circumstances, people tend to disregard the lines of respect and authority. The closer the social involvement the more the lines of distinction seem to fade and the regard of title and position seem to disappear. This becomes alarmingly true if a special incident or situation irritates one person against another. A hidden feeling is emoted and overriding the friendship of years the tolerance of suppressed resentment fails to contain the verbal expression of hostility.

Some of us experiencing this distasteful episode in our life would lash out against the perpetrator or engage in a verbal tirade of caustic words. But few would swallow their injured pride and look upon the offender with eyes of compassion and pray for them. It takes a super abundance of love to forgive a person who has publicly profaned your name, challenged your authority, and relegated the fantastic things you have done to the trash heap. It takes love to extinguish the fires of bitterness, dismiss the storm of embarrassment, and calm the turbulent sea of misunderstanding. You could crush them, smash them, and/or destroy them easily, especially when the attack was unprovoked, unwarranted and a result of prejudice.

But he who does not slumber nor sleep, who has created you to be sensitive to His will and has anointed you to represent Him in crucial, demanding situations overshadows you. He hears all that is said, sees all that is done, and occupies the sole position of making the difference. He loves you. You are special in His sight. The Psalmist says "The sun shall not smite you by day nor the moon by night; the Lord will preserve thee from all evil." Psalm 21. With this divine security we need not fear what men may say or attempt to do to us, the Lord is on our side.

Miriam, the eldest child of Jochabed and Amran, the sister of Aaron verbally tampered with her younger brother Moses' authoritative position because he married an Ethiopian woman. She was consumed with anger and bitter resentment because of this marriage and utilized conspiracy, her position in the Hebrew society, and the whip of her tongue. She failed to realize the omnipresence of God. Paul, in Acts 17:28, says "For in Him we live and move and have our being." God heard Miriam and Aaron before the door of the tabernacle and rebuked them both. Burning with anger God smote Miriam with the terminal disease of leprosy.

Moses, who was also there at the tabernacle, in a gesture of great compassion even for this woman who was willing to destroy him, pled with God for mercy in her behalf. She was guilty, convicted and sentenced by Yahweh. Other men who had drummed up sedition or the overthrow of Moses' leadership had been destroyed because of the anger of God. This was not a man. This was a woman and yet her tongue had incited many people to question not only the authority of Moses but even God's selection in choosing him. Why should she be spared? She a mere creature of the dust challenging the creator of the entire universe, the infamous insult of it, is horrendous. Moses' plea for mercy in the ears of God halted justice and halted the chosen executor, leprosy, from acting according to God's orders.

So often in life anger provokes us to do away with those controlled by the enemy to do us harm. And even though the scripture declares that vengeance belongs to God, Jesus requests us to pray for our enemies, and to do good to those who despitefully use us. Miriam put her life in jeopardy by allowing the force of evil to manipulate her to overthrow God's anointed.

GOD SAID IT AND I BELIEVE IT
Jeremiah 39:18b

Human beings say a lot of things, good and bad, that we may hear and accept based upon the credulousness of the speaker. Bitter experience has taught us not to believe everything we hear nor to accept as true every promise that is made to us. When a promise is relayed by an authentic minister of God and the promise is made by God himself, there is reason for us to accept the declaration.

Walking through the pages of ancient history, we come upon a man whose name very briefly greets us as we review the life of one prophet of Judah by the name of Jeremiah. The man to which I refer is an Ethiopian by the name of Ebed Melek, a minister of distinction serving in the cabinet of Zedekiah. Contrary to what many assume to be true, all Ethiopians were not slaves nor did they fulfill menial and subservient positions in every kingdom of yesteryear. Those who held the reigns of great nations in their hands were not concerned with the pigmentation of the skin as much as they were concerned with the intelligence and wisdom in the mind of those who aided them in guiding the destiny of their peoples. Ebed Melek shared in the administration of the kingdom of Judah and enjoyed not only the prestige of such office but his knowledge guided King Zedekiah in making decisions of significance.

It was at a time when the people of Judah desired peace but found frustration and the threat of war at their door. There is a way "that seemeth right unto man but the end thereof is death," is recorded in Proverbs 14:12. Alliances with nations whose armies have been successful in war is not always the path for nations of lesser military might to pursue. Because people are not conversant with the power of God to fight their battles and to vanquish those who would destroy, many nations are swallowed up in destruction. Israelite history enumerates many battles won by God's people because they listened to His word and obeyed His commands. The blood of thousands of warriors flowed freely on many battlefields and the people of God, though out-numbered, were victorious because God was on their side. Stranger still the victory was won and they did not have to engage in the clatter and clash of sword and spear nor in the physical contest of heated battle. The angel of God destroyed the enemy by causing them to butcher themselves or to die from the sword of disease.

Jeremiah was a fearless outspoken prophet of God who acquainted his people, the advisory council to the king, and the king himself that they could not win unless they heeded God's message. God said "you have forsaken me, you have been unfaithful to me, and unless you return I will chasten you." The people and the advisory council took exception not of God but of God's messenger, Jeremiah, and turned their hatred on Him. They wished to shut his mouth, to seal his lips, even to take his life for they did not fear God nor were they willing to receive the message He sent. Ultimately they persuaded King Zedekiah to surrender Jeremiah into their hands declaring him a traitor worthy of death. They put him in a dry cistern hoping this temporary confinement would result in his death.

One hymn writer has penned these lines, "The Lord moves in mysterious ways, His wonders to perform." Ebed Melek made sensitive to the plight of Jeremiah by the power of God, prevailed upon the king to rescue him from his tomb of death. Zedekiah empowered Ebed Melek to deliver Jeremiah from his place of confinement and to give him bread to eat as long as it was available. Because Ebed Melek feared God and recognized that Jeremiah had been unjustly accused and punished, he jeopardized his own life to exonerate Jeremiah. Because he had delivered the human median from which God had spoken, God Almighty made him a promise. God told Jeremiah to tell Ebed Melek, the Cushite that, "I am going to fulfill my word against the city through disaster. But I will rescue you on that day, declares the Lord; and you will not be handed over to those whom you fear. I will save you; and you will not fall by the sword but escape with your life, because you trust in me, declares the Lord." Jeremiah 39:16–18 (NIV).

Just as Jeremiah had predicted, the Babylonian war machine of men, horses, chariots, overflowed the city and left lifeless forms of men, women, children, horses, cattle, and other animals strewed throughout the city as evidence of their assault motivated by the wrath of God. Other members of Judea were found broken in spirit, humiliated and dejected walking behind their proud Babylonian conquerors like docile cows, as slaves in route to the city of Babylon. King Zedekiah looked with horror as his sons were butchered before his eyes and as if to seal that memory forever in his mind glowing, according to Jewish tradition, an iron lance was used to blind him. The city and its inhabitants were totally devastated as evidenced by the charred ruins of areas that were once homes, places of worship and places of business. The wisp of smoke and the stench of death gave evidence of the thoroughness of the judgment of God upon the city of Jerusalem.

But God had made a promise to Ebed Melek, a promise as secure as the foundation of the world, and as certain as were God's judgment. And so this Ethiopian officer was able to view the terrible might of Yahweh as was evidenced by the fury and destruction of the Babylonian hosts. But he, an Ethiopian from the land of Cush, was not abused nor mistreated. Not a hair on his head was touched. No shackles were draped upon his wrists or ankles, no whip cut the flesh from his back. No sword drew blood from his body, nor did any spear penetrate his physical frame. In the midst of all this death and destruction God as He had promised sustained and preserved his life. He was free to leave the destroyed city of Jerusalem and journey wherever his mind might lead him. Well hath the Psalmist said "the steps of a good man are ordered by the Lord." God said it, it is well for us to believe it.

MUST JESUS BEAR THE CROSS ALONE
Matthew 27:32
Mark 15:21
Luke 23:26

The tragedy of sin is that nothing on this earth escapes its destructive power. Every creation of God in which there is life has already been touched with the venom of sin. Because of sin the ground was cursed, the animal kingdom was cursed and humankind was cursed. This we learn from Genesis 3:14 – 18. God is not frustrated in His creative ability to form rejects by his divine power. God does not make junk just for the sake of creating something. He alone has the artistic skill to form creations that continue to create and that which though formed as a single entity will germinate and multiply in endless continuance.

Because He is God, He is able to remold, reshape, modify, augment that which He has made to fulfill the ultimate destiny that He has planned for it. Man, who was a lesser being than God though invested with God-given intelligence, either destroys or in some wise alters that which he has made in the creation of objects for his own pleasure. But so often man must discard defective creations that he has made, relegate them to the junk heap, throw the metal back into the melting pot, crush the objects back to dust, and start all over again. Man has to revise the pattern and plan of the original design on the drawing board, insert a change that will supplement an undesired function. Man must begin again and again with a different dream, a different plan, a different design.

The God of all creation, because of His singular perfection, does not discard nor cast away his creations for they are not mechanical, metallic or lifeless items. Because God is God, and in the range of His visual perspective, He sees the present as well as the distant future. Unknown to mortal man God comprehends our potential from the negative to the positive, from the possibility of error to ultimate perfection. The wisdom of God gave to all people the unique gift of choice knowing that this creation might choose evil rather than good. God was conscious that the power of love, a part of Him infused in the human being would have the power to ultimately perfect His creation.

And so through forty-two generations of marred creatures made in the image and likeness of God, God brings forth one in whom He concentrates the likeness of Himself. One who is Himself, one who supernaturally incorporated Himself in human flesh and becomes what man calls the Incarnate God—Jesus Christ. Through this creation God concentrates His love that has the power to call forth from creatures made in His likeness a responding love from them. And this love initiates the power to transform them into the likeness of God. Those who write about Jesus see in Him a variety of qualities and thus they allude to Him by a variety of titles. One calls Him the anointed Messiah or the expected deliverer of Israel but it is the same manifestation of God. Another is appalled by His miracles and teachings and sees Him as the Holy Servant of God. Another views Him as being sensitive to human illnesses and disease and marvels at the compassion in Him and calls Him the Son of Man. Another caught up in the demonstration of the supernatural powers of this One, acknowledges Him as the very Son of God.

This incarnation called Jesus, is introduced to bring forth a committed love for God the Father that will cause us to totally and actively surrender ourselves to Him and to experience a total change within our inner beings. A change that balances and cancels out the defect in us caused by the intrusion of sin. To guarantee for all time and eternity the certainty of this power, to change us from the way we are to the way we must be, this incarnated form, called Jesus, must become a living sacrifice. It is only when this Jesus, the incarnation of God in human flesh, suffers, bleeds, dies and arises from the dead that the power of God's love can produce the change in the spirit, mind and body.

Jesus preached, taught, and demonstrated, to friend and foe and drew from the scriptures undeniable confirmation of His authority. The cross was not just the wood on His shoulder that He was forced to drag from the praetorium to the skull shaped hill called Golgotha. The cross of wood is but a symbol of the real cross that Jesus bore. The real cross is the love of God imploring the mind of men and women surrounded by a wall of hate, greed, suspicion, disbelief, fear, resentment, lies, and of self-righteousness. It is only when God's love enters the mind that perfection can begin to be realized. The imperfect becomes perfect, the unclean can be made clean, the unholy holy, the unrighteous, righteous only through the love of God.

Each one of us who have not only accepted the Lord Jesus but have committed our lives to Him, help Jesus bear his cross like Simon the Cyrenian. It is not the ruthless Roman soldier who commands us to get under the cross that Jesus bears but rather it is the love of God that constrains us to do so. What we feel in our hearts as we look at wasted lives of young people, dope addicts, the homeless, those involved in self-destruction compels us to bear the cross of Jesus. We judge not to condemn but we do judge to see the brevity of time and the needless waste of that which cannot be reclaimed or recalled. We help Jesus bear the cross through the walls of resentment, prejudice, bigotry, arrogance, that also blind the sight as well as the heart.

Persons can become so confident and satisfied in the walled city of their mind that they are deceived to believe that wrong is right and right is wrong. We need to help Jesus bear the cross. The ignorance of God's mercy and love is a scheme perpetrated by the adversary to increase the candidates that go to the broadway of destruction and to decrease the few that walk the narrow path toward righteousness with God. We need to help Jesus bear the cross for one day someone motivated by the love of God assaulted our mind with the word of truth, made a breach in the wall surrounding our mind and let the love of God enter in.

Pity makes us feel sorry for those who are hurting and for those who are in need but the love of God in our hearts and minds moves us to bear the cross with Jesus and lead someone to the saving knowledge of Him who died that all people might believe and be saved.

SERMON STARTERS

I.

There are a host of issues addressed in the text about Noah and Ham and its interpretation which merit the serious attention of the preacher and Bible teacher. These include:

beastiality/sodomy	projection of responsibility
depravity (of the enemy)	subjective interpretations
drunkenness	edibility for power
ethnic stereotyping	legitimation of a hero
modesty	pigmentocracy
sin of racism	political subjugation
religious lies	sin as accidental
slavery as sin	victimization

II.

An issue stemming from the Hagar story is that Yahweh, the creator of the entire universe, and everything that is contained therein, even to the most detailed infinitesimal form of life is also a God of mercy and compassion. He may not prevent the creatures made in His image and likeness from demonstrating their acts of inhumanity against other human individuals, but He does mollify and lessen the intensity of pain that we cause each other by what we say, what we do, and the vengeance we heap on each other. This gracious characteristic of God's divine nature is vividly demonstrated in the life of Hagar, the Egyptian female bond-slave of Sarai.

Sarai demonstrated impatience characteristic of human nature unable to wait for God's 'fullness of time'. The inference is demonstrated here that God needs help, He can't fulfill His promise, or that there was a need to assist God into fulfilling a promise He has made. Our finite thinking does not permit us to see the length, the

breadth, nor the depth of our human traversity of time in the realm
of the supernatural. Our limited thinking circumscribed in its entirety
by the immediate present, cannot discern the ramifications of the
distant future. Our mind is caught up in its own self-importance and
the egocentric trip on which we propel our desires, brings diverse
anguish and sometimes pain to the incidental creatures that we
involve in our fantasy. David became inflamed with the physical
beauty of Bathsheba, and his unrestrained passion led to treachery,
deceit, betrayal, enticement, and ultimately death for the man whose
wife he had violated, (II Samuel 11:1–17). Sarai caught up in the
light of her own inadequacy set the stage for the abuse and misuse
of another human being to satisfy her ignorance of the power of
God. Before this story concludes, two people will suffer as innocent
victims of Sarai's impatience.

This is not a story that reflects the qualities that supposedly are to
reside in the lives of God-fearing people, or those who extol the
qualities of religious people, for it shows the inglorious side of Sarai
and Abram. It reveals details that would cause these two people to
blush for shame and try to hide under an avalanche of excuses. Sarai
pursued the practice that is employed by a few women of today who
engage surrogate mothers to give them children by their husbands
since they are unable to have children.

Another issue: what was it that provokes Sarah to express this fear
mixed with hatred regarding Ishmael who the scripture says is only
playing? Is the scripture silent with 'the way' he played? Is the
scripture silent about 'what he said'? Is the scripture silent about
some inference or gesture he made? Or is it that from the subconscious mind of Sarah some awful brooding fire—a mixture of a
mother's desperate possessive love mixed with wild imaginative ideas
of cruelty and frenzied phantoms of diabolical torture visited upon
her son Isaac by Ishmael—that incites Sarah to demand of Abraham
that he banish Hagar and Ishmael from the home camp? Is it more
than just her jealousy for the welfare of Isaac and his inheritance
that she became obsessed with the incessant cry to Abraham to
thrust Hagar and Ishmael from the household.

Hagar had experienced slavery and the abuse that attends slavery
as it affects one with no voice, no protection and no means of
recourse. Yet with all of the abuse, discomfort and maltreatment that
a slave might experience at the hands of their master or subordinate

members of the family, they do experience an undeniable awareness of their need and importance to their masters or mistresses. There are distinct experiences where the slave may undergo physical pain that can accelerate to the point of their death but psychologically that slave still senses they are important to their personal mistress or owner.

Hagar's slavery had degenerated to the point where she was no longer wanted, considered, nor had any relative importance. She was now on a marginalized fringe of existence. She had been publicly rebuked, demoted from a concubine back to a slave and now is rejected and cast off as an unwanted object of disdain. She had been expelled, discarded, cast on the junk pile as a worthless nothing.

This marginalization is worse than slavery for it impinges upon both physical and psychological death. Psychological death destroys the worth, dignity, pride, and personal value within oneself. Because no one else wants you initiates a slow process of self-destruction, the ultimate end of which is death. Another facet of this marginalized existence is physical death.

It is extremely difficult for an individual who has been living in a society acquainted with interpersonal relationships with the give and take of human intercourse to find themselves and adjust to expulsion from a social group. The caring, the sharing, the protection is gone, and one is left a helpless, hopeless prey to whatever terminating force is on the move looking for a victim. Hagar's post-slavery exclusion was far worse than her slavery's inclusion. What a devastating climax for one who had been the daughter of a King to find herself now less than a slave, a nobody and a nothing literally thrown away from the only people that she knew.

Another theme: Hagar was desolate, frustrated and tortured with uncertainty for her future and that of her child. Hagar had been Abraham's concubine, the mother of his first-born child whom he sent away without escort or adequate supplies impelled by the demand of jealous Sarah. Abraham gave her a single skin of water and a single loaf of bread; how long would that last? How long could this sustenance keep them on their trek to an uncertain destination exposed, unprotected to nature, wild beasts, and beastly men? He had the means to be much more generous, for he was a very wealthy man and could have provided lavishly for his offspring and the mother of his first child. As a patriarch and a prince he did not deal fairly, mercifully, justly, rightly with those who were so close to him.

Playing hide and seek among the customs of the east, putting on the veneer of wisdom and solemnity and playing with Hebrew tradition, Abraham is really involved in a monstrous act. This physically exhausted mother and child, broken-hearted and overcome with a feeling of rejection, lay down beneath the shade of one of the sparse and rare shrubs that would shield mother and son from the relentless burning rays of the desert sun. The bread and the water is gone, and the effects of dehydration drain the life from the young lad, Ishmael. The young child pleads for water but there is no water. Weak with exhaustion and growing delirious with fever, the young lad writhes as the body endeavors to gain freedom from the encroaching pangs of death.

Helplessly, Hagar, unable to listen to the desperate plea arising from the parched lips of her son, withdraws a short distance from where he lay, and yet not far enough away to abandon him to his fate. Somewhere deep from within his being, say his subconscious mind, the teaching about Yahweh, the observed practice of the worship of Yahweh, the prayers for help and deliverance came into focus. The lips that had never prayed before, the mouth that had never uttered the name of God, the spirit that never before reached out to its creator, now pleads for mercy. Hagar, the lad's mother, also pleads for mercy amid tears of maternal anguish; she knew unless God intervened, her son would soon be dead. In her desperation she grasped for any supernatural help that she could obtain.

Although she had observed her former master and mistress involved in the worship of Yahweh, her present circumstances gave her no consolation that her help would come from this God. She thought about the Gods of Egypt from whose communication she had been away from for many years. Her subconscious mind led her in this strange land to implore their intercession in this her desperate time of need. Genesis 21:17 says, "And God heard the voice of the lad; and the angel of God called to Hagar out of heaven, and said unto her, What aileth thee, Hagar? Fear not; for God has heard the voice of the lad where he is. Arise, lift up the lad and hold him in thine hand; for I will make him a great nation." Hagar captivated by fear terrorized by her helplessness on this vast desert, and mentally destruct by her attending circumstances, was an easy prey to the multiple powers of fear. Fear immobilized her so that she was unable to move. Fear *numbed* her mind, preventing rational intelligent thinking. Fear numbed her ears so that natural sounds were muted. Fear blinded her eyes so that she could not discern natural phenomena before her.

Somehow in our most desperate state Gods voice can be heard. I Kings 19:11 & 12, Elijah had reached Horeb, the mountain of God, and needed to receive a word of encouragement from Yahweh. Three natural phenomena took place, first was a great and powerful wind that tore the mountains apart and shattered the rocks before the Lord. The second was a devastating earthquake which caused the earth to tremble and to shake as if it were experiencing death throws. The third was a fire that burned with intensive consuming heat but the last phenomena was a still small voice, a gentle whisper that spoke to him. Within the auditory chambers of the conscious intelligent understanding of Hagar God spoke to her. God dispelled the fear that had blinded her, it caused her to open her eyes and to see a well of water that she had never seen before. The scripture says she went and filled the skin with water and gave to the boy to drink. This revived the lad, spared his life, and enabled them to complete their journey to Paran. The destiny of Ishmael as relayed to Hagar by God was fulfilled. "They that call upon the name of the Lord shall be delivered." (Joel 2:32 KJV)

III.

The issue addressed in the text about the Danites and the Falasha is as follows: according to the legend, the Danites refused to fight against their brethren, even at the request of a the king. They were not pacifists, for they fought against Sisera and later in Ethiopia. But they did no violence in the family!

IV.

Three issues addressed in the text about Ebed Melek include: (1) The Rehabilitation of an Ancient Heroic Cushite. There are many attempts currently going to rehabilitate yesterday's "bad guys," e.g.,

Mudd (who medically treated C. W. Booth, Lincoln's assassin) and Rudolf Hauptmann, the kidnapper of Charles Lindbergh's son. How much more the need to rehabilitate one of Israel's most unique heroes—the *one* Gentile, who along with *one* Jew, was guaranteed personal safety when Jerusalem fell in 587 B. C. Ebed Melek put his life on the line, if not for Yahweh, for Jeremiah and the truths Jeremiah stood for. In being prepared to lose his life, he found it!

(2) Resident aliens and outsiders may have an eye and ear for the truth when the insiders are blind and deaf to the obvious. Ebed Melek, the Cushite, placed a value on truth which few Judean politicians, priests, prophets, or people could match. He acted on what he believed, risking everything.

(3) Whereas ancient Judeans were prejudiced against Jeremiah (a prejudice against a prophet who was thought to be unpatriotic in the same way that other Judeans were), Euro-Americans for a millennium have been racially prejudiced against a Judean-Cushitic hero. Ancient Judeans wanted Jeremiah dead; but Euro-Americans and Afro-Americans as well, have been satisfied to leave Ebed Melek dead and forgotten. While rabbinic tradition elevated Ebed Melek to the realm of heaven, the Christian tradition—Black and White, African and American—have relegated him to oblivion. In a contemporary society that is searching for male role models, Ebed Melek needs to be resurrected in our Christian consciousness.

V.

From the story of Simon of Cyrene the following issues emerge. Sometimes we are caught up in circumstances in strange or unusual conditions that we have not orchestrated nor provoked into existence that have far-reaching affects upon us, our future or upon others. The telling fact is not that we are faced with these experiences but rather what we do when we are involved in these experiences. Like Simon, we may be thrust without warning, preparation or previous knowledge into a place of unusual greatness, or to share in magnificent greatness. We may have the opportunity to withdraw, to voice opposition, to register our disapproval. The Master of all time and of all life grants us the opportunity to share with him on occasions of unfolding the magnificence of His supernatural events in life. We will never have a second opportunity nor be able to replay what we failed to do. Today, now, the opportunity presents itself. What are we going to do with what God has given us?

CONCLUSIONS

In the light of the exegetical investigation presented in this thesis essay concerning Blacks in the Bible, I have come to the following conclusions:

1. The Bible is not silent nor does it ignore the contributions that Blacks have made to the redemptive story of the human family. The evidence is there in the Word but is not as obvious to the eye of the human reader who peruses the Sacred Word, that the sons and daughters from Africa have a dynamic message to give to all of Adam's posterity.

2. To make the characters who represent the Black members of the family of God less strange to our ear and eye, some mediums should be developed to make their life and historical input more familiar to the Biblical reader. These mediums could take on the form of drama, novels, games, calendars, or any medium that would attract the eye or the ear of people in general.

3. The repeated use of the names of Ebed-Melech, Tharbis, Hagar, and Falashas, in conversation or illustrative material employed in speeches or sermons could help acquaint the listening public of their value and existence through our communication. We who are knowledgeable have the responsibility of passing on what we have discovered to those who are yet in the darkness of ignorance.

4. These people of color experience the same social problems that are currently experienced by people in our society, in our world, in this country, and all ethnic groups today. Their situation lived in the past is a part of the current issues that face us now. Although we are removed from the chronological period in history, and although we are well advanced beyond them in creature comforts, human nature is still the same. God's mercy is available to those that call on the Name of the

Lord. Thus the story of the Bible can never be relegated to ancient history nor shrouded in the grave clothes of what 'used to be' but is alive and current in today's ledger of life.

ENDNOTES

1.   Volume I (650 pages) was published in 1987 by Free Association Press; Volume II (735 pages) appeared in 1991, published by Rutgers University Press. Bernal lamented that professional reviewers turned down the publication project for volume two. But Kenneth Arnold, the Director of Rutgers University Press decided (with the enthusiastic backing of Leslie Mitchner, the Humanities Editor) to use his right to publish three books a year without going through the normal professional reviewing process in order to accept *Black Athena* unconditionally.

2.   Currently the Black Yahwists (Black Hebrew Israelites) are facing serious legal problems.   Donna Gehrke reported in the *Philadelphia Inquirer* on January 3, 1992, that sixteen members of the group, including their leader Yahweh ben Yahweh, were on trial, accused of conspiracy in the deaths of fourteen people.

3. A film has also been produced which presents the pros and cons of Bernal's *Black Athena*.   For a classicist's response to Bernal's theories and those of other Afro-centrists, see Lefkowitz 1992: 29–36.

4.   Felder (1989: 38–40) used the term sacralization to convey the concept of "transporting an ideological concept into a tenet of religious faith in order to serve the vested interest of a particular ethnic group." An example of this sacralization according to him, is brought in the Old Testament. He states:

> It is in Genesis 9:18–27, which has achieved notoriety in many quarters because it contains so-called curse of Ham. Technically the passage should follow directly after the quote "J" passage that concludes the flood narrative of Genesis 8:20–22, since critical investigations have shown that Genesis 9:1–17, 28, 29, represent the much later Priestly ("P") exilic tradition. The great significance of Genesis 9:18–27 is not that it contains the so-called curse of Ham, which technically does not take place at all. Rather these verses make it clear that, to the mind of the ancient Israelite author, "the whole post-diluvial humanity stems from Noah's three sons" (p. 39). Claus Westermann remarks on Genesis 9:19, "the whole of humanity takes its origin from them (Shem, Ham, Japheth)... humanity is conceived here as a unity, in a way different from the creation; humanity in all its variety across the earth, takes it origin

from these three who survive the flood.   The purpose of the contrast is to underscore the amazing fact that humanity scattered in all its variety throughout the world comes from one family."

Felder suggests that there was a breach in the moral respect that Ham had for his father, Noah, which was vital in the social tenets of the day. A later version of the story, that was motivated by political developments in ancient Palestine, attempted to justify Shem's descendants (Israel) and those Japheth (Philistines) over the subjugated Canaanites. Westermann in his commentary on Genesis states "the same person who committed the outrage in verse 22 falls under the curse in verse 25. The Yahwist has preserved, together with the story of Ham's outrage a curse over Canaan which could be resumed because of the genealogical proximity of Canaan to Ham. Those who heard the story knew the descendants of Ham as identical with those of Canaan (Cush, Egypt, Put/Punt).

Felder suggested that the ambiguity of the text can lead biblical interpreters to justify their interpretation of a particular history, culture or race by using theological passages that justify their thinking. He noted:

> The idea that the blackness of the Africans was due to a curse and thus reinforced and sanctioned in slaving blacks, persisted into the 17th century. In *Dake's Annotated Reference Bible*, one can find in Genesis 9:18–27 the so-called "great racial prophesy" with the following racial hermeneutic:

> "All colors and types of men came into existence after the flood. All men were white up to this point, for there was only one family line of Christ being mentioned in Luke 3:36 with the son Shem...prophesy that Shem would be a chosen race and have peculiar relationship with God. All divine revelation since Shem has come through his line... prophesy and Japheth would be the father of the great and enlarged races. Government, Science, Art are mainly Japhethic . . . . His descendants constitute the leading nations of civilization."

5. Republished in *Slavery Defended: the Views of the Old South*, edited by Eric L. McKitrick, Englewood Cliffs, NJ: Prentice Hall, 1963, 86–98, with full notation on the original publication. For other literature of the time defending slavery see Swartley 1983: 30–37.

6. Note especially one of his closing comments:

Despite the New World's history of exclusive black slavery, patterns of race relations have arisen there that share an underlying common feature with those of the Muslim world of the Near East and North Africa: each of these societies is a *pigmentocracy*, ruled by people with light skin. This racial distribution of power, established centuries ago by the clash of arms, is maintained by a system of color values that permits a governing elite to define eligibility to power and privilege in its own image. Such color values are expressed in a cluster of distance-creating ideas, ideas that attach characteristics to the Negro that were *once attached to slaves of any origin* and that make a caricature of the physical and cultural traits of sub-Saharan Africans. (italics mine)

7. The work of Rosenberg and Bloom has received very poor reviews by many biblical scholars, most of which are all well summarized in the stinging review by Cooper and Goldstein (1991: 45-60).

8. Though Rosenberg cites no references, one can note, for example, Sarna 1989: 64.

9. To "see someone's nakedness" is a way of referring to sexual intercourse with one's wife and does not describe homosexual relationship but heterosexual relationship, even when it speaks of seeing another man's nakedness (see, for example, Lev. 18: 14). Thus, "to see the nakedness of your father" really means "to see the nakedness of your mother," whether she is your maternal mother or your step-mother or even your father's concubine as was in the case in Jacob's family. Leviticus 20 specifically states that if someone lays with or takes someone's wife, he has "uncovered that man's nakedness."

It is, therefore, not difficult for us to interpret logically the statement that Ham *saw* the nakedness of his father to originally have meant that he had sexual intercourse with his father's wife. Were this the case, we can understand the intensity of the curse. This could explain why Noah cursed one of Ham's sons rather than all of Ham's sons, especially if Canaan was the result of that incestuous act. This possibility seems to justify Noah's curse on Canaan for something that his father Ham did. Canaan would have been the offspring of Ham's violation of Noah's wife. The story, then, would run parallel to the Old Testament story dealing with Reuben's incestuous relationship with Bilhah, the concubine of his father Jacob. Because of this the descendants of Reuben lost their natural place of preference in Israel that was afforded the first born (Genesis 35:22; 49:3 – 4). In the Noah tradition the incestuous act would result in the genealogical line of Noah being altered to remove Ham from the person second in line to receive family preference to the last position, to that of the youngest son.

A second demonstration of intense rebuke due to conception out of wedlock was the death of the offspring of David's illicit act with Bathsheba, the wife of Uriah (II Samuel 12:15). The curse of slavery for an indefinite period would rest upon the off-spring of Canaan. It may be that this is the reason the story is altered so that tradition could harmonize with the second recorded biblical genealogy of Noah's off-spring being Shem, Japheth and Canaan.

However, this would mean that the biblical story is abnormally telescopic in having the child conceived, born, named, and cursed —all in the time that Noah was waking up from his drunkenness. The problem of this offense and the identity of the offender may not be conclusively satisfied by following traditional lines of interpretation.

10.   It is interesting to note, according to Bassett's investigation (1971: 236) of the Old Testament, that there are no sex laws in the Old Testament Canon which prohibit sexual relations between father and daughter.

11.   According to Genesis 17:20 and 25:12 – 16, Ishmael was the father of twelve princes and through them the father of twelve tribes. Their names are (1) Nebaioth, (2) Kedar, (3) Adbeel, (4) Mibsam, (5) Mishma, (6) Dumah, (7) Massa, (8) Hadad, (9) Tema, (10) Jetur, (11) Naphish, and (12) Kedemah.

12.   Speiser 1964: 117 called attention to the fact that the Hebrew word here is *'iššah*, the regular word for "wife" and "woman." He translated it as "concubine," however, citing the Akkadian cognate which also has the same semantic range from the English "wife" to "concubine."

13.   The text, translated by J. J. Finkelstein (1969: 542) reads as follows:

Laqipum has married Hatala, daughter of Enishru. In the country (i.e., Central Anatolia) Laqipum may not marry another (woman) — (but) in the city (i.e., Ashur) he may marry a hierodule [*qadištum*]. If within two years she (i.e., Hatala) does not provide him with an offspring, she herself will purchase a slave woman, and later on after she [i.e., either the slave woman *or* Hatala, the text is not clear] will have produced a child by him, he [she (?)] may then dispose of her by sale wheresoever he pleases. Should Laqipum choose to divorce her [text "him"], he may pay her five minas of silver; and should Hatala choose to divorce him, she must pay (him) five minas of Silver. Witnesses: Masa, Ashurishtikal, Talia, Shupianika.

14. The text, translated by Kramer in *ANET* (1955: 160) reads as follows:

If a man's wife has not borne him children (but) a harlot (from) the public square has born him children, he [the father] shall provide grain, oil, and clothing for that harlot; the children which the harlot has borne him shall be his heirs, and as long as the wife lives the harlot shall not live in the house with the wife.

Sarna also listed similar laws from the code of Hammurabi, found in

ANET 172, paragraphs 144–145.

15. But McDaniel (1992) cautions against these dates noting that Ur III is assigned the dates 2060–1950 in the Albright/ Bright chronology, while the Twelfth Dynasty is given the date of 1991–1786.

16. Teubal (1990: 49–70) has discussed in great detail the precise meaning of the Hebrew term *shifḥah* "handmaid, maidservant" used with reference to Hagar. In addition to emphasizing that Hagar was the handmaid of Sarah, not the concubine of Abraham, Teubal listed the following:

1.   Hagar was Sarah's *shifḥah*.

2.   She becomes Abraham's second wife.

3.   Hagar's sexual services are controlled by her mistress.

4.   Her progeny will belong to her mistress.

5.   She is harshly punished because she does not conform to her mistress's wishes.

6.   Hagar is seemingly not in control of her own destiny.

7.   Hagar changes from being the *shifhah* of Sarah to becoming the *amah* ["maid"] of Abraham.

8.   Finally, Hagar is regarded solely as the mother of a son of Abraham's: Because of the Patriarch, this son of Hagar is blessed by God as ancestor of a people, who are albeit the enemies of the Israelites.

17. It is also of note in this same article that foreign slaves remained slaves in perpetuity, whereby Hebrew slaves could recover their liberty in the year of jubilee (a national observance instituted in the Levitical law to be observed every fifty years, which granted freedom to Hebrew slaves. Alienated lands were to be returned and fields were left uncultivated to rest from production for one year.)

18. See Hackett *Rehabilitating Hagar: Fragments of Epic Pattern* (1989: 12–27) and von Rad, *Genesis* (1956: 186).

19. Note the familiar stories of how Cain supplanted Abel and Jacob supplanted Esau.

20. The appearing of the angel of the Lord in the Old Testament is called theophany. It is considered as the visible appearance of the Son of God prior to the incarnation.

21. Cited from William Whiston's translation, *The Works of Josephus*, Volume II, *The Antiquity of the Jews*, 161–162. Grand Rapids: Baker Book House, 1974 reprint.

22. The identification of Kush with the Kushan of Midian precludes another possibility. Albright (1968: 205) also listed a place in northern Syria by the name Kūšǎn-rōm, "high-Kushan" (mentioned in texts of the 13–12 centuries B. C.), which could also be a by-form of the original Kūš. The relation of this Cush/Cushan with the Kassites known from Mesopotamia in the sixteenth century B. C. remains problematic.

23. Milgrom noted that the first word of Numbers 12:1 in the Hebrew is in the feminine form, indicating that Miriam was the primary instigator of the gossip against Moses, and as a result she— not Aaron—was punished.

24. It is believed that about 5,000–4,000 B. C. a phenomenon called the Flandrian Transgression caused a sudden rise in the sea level. The gulf began to fill with water and actually reached its present day level. Eden was inundated, and the effects of the catastrophe continued northward into the southern regions of modern day Iraq and Iran.

25. This citation and those that follow are from Felder 1989: 25.

26. This is also cited by Felder 1989: 26.

27. See Van Beek 1962: 145 (cited by Felder as a contribution of Buttrick, rather than Van Beek.)

28. See Carl Bezold, editor, *The Kebra Nagast*, 1905, pp. 11–173.

29. See Gordon 1962 and Albright 1962.

30. See *The Kebra Nagast*, pp. 61–64.

31. The term Shulammite appears to be the feminine form of Shulman, i.e. Solomon "man of peace"; whereas the terms Shunam-mite refers to one from the town of Shunem in Issachar (Josh. 19:18), which has been identified with the village of Solem over-looking the valley of Jezreel.

32. Pope (1977: 308) noted that in modern Israeli Hebrew the word Cushite is still employed with derogatory and racist overtones. Persons who have a feeling of appreciation for their blackness, obviously, have not registered any negative prejudice for the phrase "black and beautiful." Pope cited, by way of example, the "Commandment Keepers" and the "Black Jews" of Harlem. Rabbi Wentworth A. Matthew, who believes he is in the ancestral line of Solomon and the Queen of Sheba, asserts that Ham and Sheba were

Black but only Japeth related to the Gentiles was White. Jacob, he says, was also Black because he had smooth skin.

33. Pope (1977: 313) noted that the oriental origin of the Black Virgin seemed to Durand-Lefebvre to be the result of clergy from the Eastern Churches who might have brought back these black statues and paintings to Rome between the sixth and twelfth centuries when the iconoclastic quarrels where in progress or in Constantinople was captured by the Turks. The pilgrims or crusaders are also a possible reason for their presence in Rome. Aphrodite was worshipped in black form as Aphrodite *melainis*, and Pausanias suggests that it was because mankind usually made love at night.

34. See Pope 1977: 314. For the text itself, see Solomon Buber 1894, 250. Note also Ginzberg 1909–1928, volume III, 352 and volume VI, 120, note 715. The Goddess of the Eastern Semites had a masculine form to the name of Ishtar. I Kings 11:7 states that Solomon built a high place (*bamah*) for Chemosh on a mountain facing Jerusalem which remained until it was destroyed by Josiah at the same time a shrine to Ashtart was destroyed in the same general area (II Kings 23:13).

35.   Other items of note in Pope's commentary include the following: Isaac of Antioch states that the pagan Arabs worshipped the Venus star under the title of Al-'Uzza, "the strong (female)," whom the Syrian women climbing to the roof tops of their houses sought in prayer to make them beautiful. It is told that one of this Goddesses chief shrines was in Nakhli which was a few miles north of Mecca. Muhammad in the eighth year after the flight to Mecca, sent a stalwart warrior named Khalid to destroy this place of worship. While in the process of destroying the last three acacia trees which were of importance to the Goddess "a naked black woman with flowing hair stood before him." She was accompanied "by a priest of this cult who cried out: 'be courageous, Al-'Uzza, and protect yourself'." The warrior smitten with terror, with a single stroke split her head and she turned into a black cinder. (From Wakidi, cited by Wellhausen, Muhammad in Medina, 351; cf. Tor Andrae, 1935, 18.) The black woman evidently represented the black goddess.

The most notorious of all black goddesses is Kali of India whose worship under many different names and aspects is endemic and especially developed in Bengal. Animal sacrifices are daily offered in her temple. The name Kali means "Black." She is beautiful, ever young, virginal, horrendous, violent, destructive, insatiable in her thirst for blood, flesh, wine and sexual intimacy. It is stated that her color varies depending upon the activity with which she is engaged. In giving liberation she is white; as controller of women, men and kings she is red; as controlling wealth she is saffron; provoking enmity she is tawny; experiencing the thrill of love and passion, she is rose colored; and in the action of killing, she becomes black (cf. A.and E. Avalon, 1952, 7-8).

36. Gordon cited Ugaritic text 51: VIII: 1, *idk al ttn pnm 'm ğr* "then surely set face toward the mountain."

37. The heroic military valor of the Danites can be found in the Song of Deborah as translated by McDaniel (1983: 218-219). He translated Judges 5:17-23 as follows:

> Gilead in Trans-Jordan was on alert. Then Dan boldly attacked the ships; Asher assailed along the water's edge and struck against its harbors. Zebulun swam immersed, risked his life, while Naphtali moved violently against Merom.

According to McDaniel, it is difficult to understand how Dan could ever have been held in high esteem for military valor if the traditional translations of this part of the Song of Deborah is correct. Note the translation in the NRSV:

> Gilead stayed beyond the Jordan; and Dan, why did he abide with the ships? Asher sat still at the edge of the sea, settling down by his landings. Zebulun is a people that scorned death; Naphtali too, on the heights of the field.

38. For a study of *falasha* and its confusion with the name "Philistine," see McDaniel 1983: 95-105.

39. For other details, see *The Philadelphia Inquirer*, May 27, 1991; *The New York Times*, May 26, 1991; and *Time*, June 3, 1991, p. 36.

40. See Brown, Driver, and Briggs, *Hebrew Lexicon*, 710a.

41.   Oppenheim 1955, cited from *Ancient Near Eastern Texts Relating to the Old Testament*, 293.

42. See the study of Mazar (1963: 310–320) in which he examines the use of "the thirty" in premonarchic biblical texts such as Judges 4:11; 10:4, 30; 12:9, 30; 14:11; and I Samuel 9:22. He noted that Ramasses III had "30" among his immediate attendants.

43. A further statement of Evans (1980: 23) is worth quoting since it indicates indirectly how late came the stereotyping of blackness with slavery. He noted:

> In response to patterns of political disorder or military conquest, however, the principal source of European slaves kept shifting, and early ethnic stereotypes lost all credibility. Various Western European nationalities at times became important sources of slaves, although not for a long enough period for any of them to acquire a slavish reputation. Gaul, for example, was an important source immediately after the Roman conquest in the first century B. C. And political and ethnic fragmentation of Britain, following the collapse of Roman power, briefly created a surplus of slaves for export in that country. In the later Middle Ages, as stable governments emerged in the West, the source of European slaves became confined increasingly to the lands around the Black Sea, areas that continued to feed the Mediterranean slave trade from remote antiquity down to the beginning of modern times.

44. See Jastrow 1903: 1003: 875 and Gordon 1965: 441, no. 1609.

45.   Herbert Wolf and John Stek, also contributors for the NIV (1985), suggested that this passage is the fourth and longest servant song of Isaiah. Although it has strong suggestive passages to the substitutionary and sacrificial sufferings of the Lord Jesus Christ, it really speaks about another human servant of God and not the only begotten Son of God.

It is the New Testament Church that takes the Isaiah 53 and fleshes it out to become a description of Jesus Christ and the time of His passion and suffering for the sins of mankind. It is this passage which is quoted more frequently in the New Testament and the New Testament Church than any other passage in the Old Testament scriptures.

Munch (1967: 78) stated that the primitive church did not feel the same inclination as later generation of Christian to apply this text to Jesus, but this is done in Philip's answer when the Ethiopian asked the same question which has been steadily repeated right up to our own time: "Does the prophet in this passage speak of himself or another?"

46.   The sudden disappearance of Philip in this incident is reminiscent of the story in the Old Testament of Elijah—even to the selection of the words that were used. Compare II Kings 2:12. (e.g., the eunuch did not see him again).

BIBLIOGRAPHY

Adamo, David Tuesday. 1986. *The Place of Africa and Africans in the Old Testament and Its Environment.* Ann Arbor, Michigan: University Microfilms International.

Albright, William F. 1941. "The Land of Damascus Between 1850 and 1750 B. C." *Bulletin of the American Schools of Oriental Research* 83: 30–36.

Albright, William F. 1962. *Peake's Commentary on the Bible.* New York: Thomas Nelson and Sons.

Albright, William F. 1968. *Archaeology and the Religion of Israel.* Fifth edition. Baltimore: Johns Hopkins University.

Baldwin, John D. 1874. *Prehistoric Nations.* New York: Harper & Brothers.

Bassett, Frederick W. 1971. "Noah's Nakedness and the Curse of Canaan: A Case of Incest," *Vetus Testamentum* 21: 232–239.

Beam, Alex. 1991. "Africa May Hold Truth about Western Roots." *Philadelphia Inquirer*, August 22.

Bennett, Robert. 1971. "Africa and the Biblical Period." *Harvard Theological Review* 64: 483–500.

Bernal, Martin. 1987. *Black Athena: The Afroasiatic Roots of Classical Civilization.* Volume I: *Greece 1785–1985.* Free Association Press.

Bernal, Martin. 1991. *Black Athena: The Afroasiatic Roots of Classical Civilization*. Volume II: *The Archaeological and Documentary Evidence*. New Brunswick, New Jersey: Rutgers University Press.

Bergsma, Stewart. 1932. *Rainbow Empire: Ethiopia Stretches Out Her Hands*. Grand Rapids: Eerdmans Publishers.

Bettenhausen, Elizabeth. 1987. *Christianity and Crisis: A Christian Journal of Opinion* 47: 157–159.

Bezold, Carl, ed. 1905. *The Kebra Nagast: Geez Text, Edited from the Original Manuscript*. Berlin, London, Oxford, Paris: Munich.

Bloom, Harold. 1990. See Rosenberg, David and Harold Bloom. 1990. *The Book of J.*

Breasted, James H. 1912. *The History of Egypt from the Earliest Times to the Persian Conquest*. New York: Charles Scribner's Sons.

Bright, John. 1965. *Jeremiah*. Anchor Bible 21. Garden City, New York: Doubleday.

Brodie, Thomas L. 1986. "Towards Unraveling the Rhetorical Imitation of Sources in Acts: 2 Kgs 5 as One Component of Acts 8, 9–40." *Biblica* 67: 41–67.

Budge, E. A. W. 1929. *A History of Ethiopia, Nubia and Abyssinia*. Volume 1. London: Methuen and Company.

Budge, E. A. W., translator. 1922. *The Kebra Nagast*.

Calkins, R. 1930. *Jeremiah The Prophet*. New York: MacMillian Company.

Carter, Leroy. 1989. *Black Heroes of the Bible*. Columbus, Georgia: Brentwood Christian Press.

Clark, John Hendrick. 1978. "New Introduction," *The Culture Unity of Black Africa*. Edited by C. A. Depot. Chicago: Third World Press.

Cooper, Alan and Bernard. R. Goldstein. 1991. "Biblical Literature in the Iron(ic) Age: Reflections on Literary-Historical Method." *Hebrew Studies* 33: 45–60.

Cooper, Len. 1991. "Biblical Scholars Aim to Show African Influence in a New Light." *Washington Post*, September 14, 1991.

Cowley, A. 1920. "A Hittite Word in Hebrew." *The Journal of Theological Studies* 21: 326–327.

Creecy, Howard W. 1978. *Aunt Hagar and Her Children*. Edited by Henry J. Young. Philadelphia: Fortress Press. 34–40.

Cross, Frank M. 1973. *Canaanie Myth and Hebrew Epic: Essays in the History of the Religion of Israel*. Cambridge, Massachusetts: Harvard University Press.

Dahood, Mitchell. 1964. "Hebrew-Ugaritic Lexicography." *Biblica* 45: 393–412.

Dake, Finis Jennings. 1981. *Dake's Annotated Reference Bible*. Lawrenceville, Georgia: Dake's Bible Sale, Inc.

De Meester, Paul. 1981. "Philippe et l'eunuque ethiopien ou 'le bapteme d'un pelerin de nubie'?" *Nouvelle Revue Theologique* 103: 360–374.

De Vaux, Roland. 1961. *Ancient Israel*. New York: McGraw Hill.

Diop, Cheirh Anta. 1974. *The African Origin of Civilization*. Translated by Mercer Cook. New York: Lawrence Hill Company.

Doi, A. R. I. 1970. "A Muslim-Christian-Traditional Saint in Yorubaland." *Practical Anthropology* 17: 261–268.

Dunstan, Alfred G. 1974. *The Black Man in the Old Testament.* Philadelphia: Dorrance and Company.

Eskin, Rachael. 1991. *The Beta-Israel: The Development Identity in the Ethiopian context,* Unpublished Thesis. University of Rochester.

Evans, William McKee. 1980. "From the Land of Canaan to the Land of Guinea: The Strange Odyssey of the 'Sons of Ham'." *The American Historical Review* 85: 15–43.

Felder, Cain Hope. 1989. *Troubling Biblical Waters.* Maryknoll, New York: Orbis Books.

Fensham. F. C. 1969. "The Son of the Handmaid." *VT* 19: 312–321.

Finkelstein, J. J. 1969. "Additional Mesopotamian Legal Documents." In *Ancient Near Eastern Texts Relating to the Old Testament*: Third Addition with Supplement, 542–547. Princeton: Princeton University Press. (Cited as *ANET Supplement.*)

Gehrke, Donna. 1992. "Miami Sect on Trial in Deaths of 14 People." *Philadelphia Inquirer,* January 3.

Ginzberg, Louis. 1909–1938. *Legends of the Jews.* 7 volumes. Philadelphia: Jewish Publication Society of America.

Gordon, Cynthia. 1985. *Hagar: A Throwaway Character Among the Matriarchs?* Society of Biblical Literature: Seminar Papers. 271–277.

Gordon, C. H. 1955. "Homer and the Bible." *Hebrew Union College Annual* 26: 43–108.

Gordon, C. H. 1965. *Ugaritic Testbook*. Rome: Pontifical Biblical Institute.

Grassi, Joseph M. 1964. "Emmaus Revisited (Luke 24, 13–35 and Acts 8, 26–40)." *Catholic Biblical Quarterly* 26: 463–467.

Gray, John. 1970. *I and II Kings*. Old Testament Library. Philadelphia: Westminster

Hackett, Jo Ann. 1989. *Rehabilitating Hagar: Fragments of An Epic Pattern*. 12–27. Edited by Peggy L. Day. Philadelphia: Fortress Press.

Hamblin, Dora Jane. 1987. "Has the Garden of Eden Been Located at Last?" *Smithsonian* 18: 127–135.

Haygood, Atticus Greene. 1895. "A Loaf and A Bottle to Hagar." *Methodist Quarterly Review*: 301–315.

Hess, Robert. 1969. "Toward a History of the Falasha." In *Eastern Africa History*. Edited by McCall et al. New York: Frederick A. Prager.

Hoftijzer, J. 1958. "Some remarks to the Tale of Noah's Drunkenness." In B. Gemser, et. al., *Studies on the Book of Genesis*, Oudtestamentische Studien, 12: 22–27. Leiden: Brill.

Irvine, A. K. 1985. "On The Identity of the Habashat in the South Arabian Inscriptions." *Journal of Semetic Studies* 10: 181.

Jastrow, Marcus. 1903. *A Dictionary of the Targumim, the Talmud Babli and Yerushalmi, and the Midrashic Literature*. New York: G. P. Putnam's Sons.

Jones, H. L., ed. and trans. 1949. *The Geography of Strabo*. The Loeb Classical Edition. Cambridge, Massachusetts: Harvard University Press.

Josephus. See William Whiston.

Kaplan, Steven. 1985. "The Falasha and the Stephanite: An Episode from Gadla Gabra Masih." *Bulletin of the School of Oriental and African Studies* 48: 2.

Kaplan, Steven. 1987. "The Beta-Israel (Falasha) in the Ethiopian Context." In *Ethiopian Jews and Israel*. Edited by Michael Ashekenazi and Alex Weingrod. Oxford: Transaction Books.

Karay, Diane. 1986. "Out of The Shadows: Hagar's Story." *The Christian Ministry* 17: 33–34.

Kealey, S. P. 1982. *Mark's Gospel: A History of Interpretation*. Philadelphia: Fortress Press.

Kee, H. C. 1962. "Niger." In *Interpreter's Dictionary of the Bible*. Volume 3: 549. G. A. Buttrick, et. al. editors. New York and Nashville: Abingdon Press.

Kodell, Jerome. 1978. "The Celibacy Logion in Matthew 19:12." *Biblical Theology Bulletin* 8: 1923.

Kramer, Samuel Noah. 1955. "Lipit-Ishtar Law Code." In *Ancient Near Eastern Texts Relating to the Old Testament*. Edited by James B. Pritchard. Princeton: Princeton University Press. 159–161. (Cited as *ANET*.)

Lee, G. M. 1975. "Mark 15:21, 'The Father of Alexander and Rufus'." *Novum Testamentum* 17: 303.

Lefkowitz, Mary. 1992. "Not out of Africa: The Origins of Greece and the Ilusions of the Afrocentrists." *The New Republic* 206 (Number 6, February 10): 29–36.

Leslau, Wolf. 1947. "A Falasha Religious Dispute." *Proceedings of the American Academy for Jewish Research* 16: 71–95.

Lesleu, Wolf. 1974. *Falahsa Anthology*. Chicago: University of Chicago Press.

Liptzin, Sol. 1979. "Solomon and the Queen of Sheba." *Dor Le Dor* 7(4): 172–186.

Lockyer, Herbert. 1958. *All The Men of The Bible*. Grand Rapids: Zondervan Publishing House.

Macho, A. D. 1970. *Neophyti: Targum Palestinense MS de la Biblioteca Vaticana*. Volume II *Éxodo*. Madrid-Barcelona: Consejo Superior de Investigaciones Científicas.

Mann, C. S. 1986. *Mark*. Anchor Bible. Garden City, New York: Doubleday.

Margaliyot, M. 1980. "Numbers 12: the Nature of Moses' Prophecy." *Beth Mikra* 25 (81): 132–149.

Mazar, Benjamin. 1963. "The Military Elite of David." *Vetus Testamentum* 13: 310–320.

McCray, Walter Arthur. 1990a. *The Black Presence in the Bible*. Chicago: Black Light Fellowship.

McCray, Walter Arthur. 1990b. *The Black Presence in the Bible and the Table of Nations [in] Genesis* 10:1–32. Chicago: Black Light Fellowship.

McDaniel, Thomas. 1983. *Deborah Never Sang*. Jerusalem: Makor.

McDaniel, Thomas. 1992. Lectures at the Eastern Baptist Theological Seminary and private communications as the Director of this writer's "Thesis Essay."

Meek, Theophile J. 1955. "The Code of Hammurabi." In *Ancient Near Eastern Texts Relating to the Old Testament*. Princeton: Princeton University. 162–180.

Mendelsohn, I. 1962. "Slavery." In *Interpreter's Dictionary of the Bible*. Volume 4: 383–390. G. A. Buttrick, et. al. editors. New York and Nashville: Abingdon Press.

Milgrom, Jacob. 1990. *Numbers*. The JPS Torah Commentary. Philadelphia and New York: The Jewish Publication Society.

Montet, Pierre. 1968. *Egypt and the Bible*. Philadelphia: Fortress.

Munck, Johannes. 1967. *Acts of The Apostles*. Anchor Bible, Garden City, NY: Doubleday.

New International Version of the Bible. 1985. Grand Rapids: Zondervan.

Oppenheim, Leo A. 1955. "Babylonian and Assyrian Historical Texts." In *Ancient Near Eastern Texts Relating to the Old Testament*. Edited by James B. Pritchard. Princeton: Princeton University Press.

Phillips, Anthony. 1980. "Uncovering the Father's Skirt." *Vetus Testament* 30: 38–43.

Plaut, W. Gunther. 1974. *The Torah, Genesis*. New York: Union of American Hebrew Congregations.

Pope, Marvin H. 1977. *Song of Songs*. The Anchor Bible. Garden City, New York: Doubleday.

Previn, Dory. 1989. "Sheba and Solomon." *Union Seminary Quarterly Review* 43(1-4): 59-66.

Pritchard, James B. 1955. *Ancient Near Eastern Texts Relating to the Old Testament*. Princeton: Princeton University Press. (Cited as *ANET*.)

Pritchard, James B. 1969. *Ancient Near Eastern Texts Relating to the Old Testament*: Third Addition with Supplement. Princeton: Princeton University Press. (Cited as *ANET Supplement*.)

Pritchard, James, editor. 1974. *Solomon and Sheba*. London: Phaidon Press.

Quirin, J. 1977. *The Beta-Israel (Falahsa) in Ethiopian History.* Ph.D. Dissertation, University of Michigan.

Rad, Gerhard von. 1961. *Genesis.* The Old Testament Library. Philadelphia: Westminster Press.

Rappaport, Louis. 1981. *The Lost Jews: Last of the Ethiopian Falashas,* New York: Stein and Day.

Rice, Jene. 1975. "Two Black Contempories of Jeremiah." *Journal of Religious Thought* 32: 95–109. (School of Religion, Howard University, Washington, D. C.)

Robinson, Bernard P. 1989. "The Jealousy of Miriam: A Note on Num 12" *Zeitschrift fur die Alttestamentliche Wissenschaft* 101: 428-432.

Rosenberg, David and Harold Bloom. 1990. *The Book of J.* New York: Grove Weidenfeld.

Sarna, Nahum. 1989. *Genesis.* The Jewish Publication Society Torah Commentary. New York and Philadelphia: Jewish Publication Society.

Schmerler, Henrietta. 1941. "Falashas." In *The Universal Jewish Encyclopedia.* Volume 4. 234–236.

Schungel-Straumann, Helen. 1989. "Miryam: Comment Miryam fut evincee (Miriam: How Miriam Was Ousted)." *Foi et Vie* 88(5): 89-99.

Schwantes, Milton. 1988. *In Faith Born in the Sstruggle for Llife.* Edited by Kirkpatrick.

Selassie, Sergew H. 1970. "The Establishment of The Ethiopian Church." In *The Church of Ethiopia, a Panarama History and Spiritual Life.* Addis Ababa: Ethiopian Orthodox Church.

Shinnie, Margaret. 1968. *Ancient African Kingdom*. London: Edward Arnold Publishers.

Skinner, John. 1930. *A Critical and Exegetical Commentary on Genesis*. Second Edition. The International Critical Commentary. Edinburgh: T. & T. Clark.

Snowden, Frank M., Jr. 1970. *Blacks in Antiquity: Ethiopians in the Greco-Roman Experience.* Cambridge, Massachusetts: Harvard University Belknap Press.

Speiser, Ephraim. A. 1964. *Genesis*. Anchor Bible I. Garden City, New York: Doubleday.

Stern, H. A. 1968. *Wanderings Among the Falashas in Abbysinia*. London: Cass.

Strabo. See H. L. Jones.

Stringfellow, Thornton. 1856. *Scriptural and Statistical Views in Favor of Slavery*. In *Slavery Defended: the Views of the Old South*. Edited by Eric L. McKitrick. Englewood Cliffs, NJ: Prentice Hall, 1963. Pages 86–98.

Swartley, Willard M. 1983. *Slavery, Sabbath, War, and Women*. Scottsdale, PA: Herald Press.

Tamez, Elsa. 1986. *New Eyes for Reading*. Edited by J. Pobbe and B. Wartenberg-Potter.

Teubal, Savina. 1962. *Hagar the Egyptian: The Lost Tradition of the Matriarchs*. San Francisco: Harper and Row.

Tribble, 1984. *Texts of Terror*. Overtures to Biblical Theology. Philadelphia: Fortress Press.

Tuckett, C. 1983. *The Revival of the Griesbach Hypothesis*. London and New York: Cambridge University Press.

Ullendorff, E. 1960. *The Ethiopians*. London: Oxford University Press.

Ullendorff, Edward. 1962–1963. "Queen of Sheba." *Bulletin of the John Rylands Library* 45: 486–501.

Van Beek, G. W. 1962. "Sabeans." In *The Interpreters Dictionary of the Bible*. Edited by George A. Buttrick. Volume 4. 144–146. Nashville: Abingdon Press.

Van Beek, Gus W. 1967. "Monuments of Axum in Light of South Arabian Archeology." *Journal of American and Oriental Society* 87: 14.

Vaux, Roland de. 1961. *Ancient Israel*. London: Darton, Longman and Todd.

Wendt, Herbert. 1962. *It Began In Babel*. Boston: Houghton Mifflin.

Westermann, Claus. 1969. *Isaiah* 40–66. Philadelphia: Fortress Press.

Westermann, Claus. 1984. *Genesis* 1–11. Minneapolis: Augsburg Press.

Williams, Larry and Childs A. Finch. 1984. "Black Women in Antiquity." *Journal of African Civilizations*. Volume 6. Edited by Ivan Van Sertima. New Brunswick: Transaction Books.

Whiston, William. 1974. *The Works of Flavius Josephus*. 4 volumes. Grand Rapids, MI: Baker Book House. (reprint)

Wolf, Herbert and John Stek, editors. 1985. *Isaiah*. New International Version of the Bible. Grand Rapids: Zondervan.

Wurmbrand, M. 1971. "Falasha." *The Jewish Encyclopedia*. 1143–1154. New York: Prentice Hall.

Yamauchi, Edwin M. 1980. "The Archaeological Background of Nehemiah. Part 4 of Archaeological Backgrounds of the Exilic and Postexilic Era." *Bibliotheca Sacra* 137: 291–309.

Yeschaq, Archbishop. 1989. *The Ethiopian Tewahedo Church*. New York: Vantage Press.

Zwemer, Samuel M. 1950. "Hagar and Ishmael." *The Evangelical Quarterly* 30: 32–39.

Martin Luther King, Jr. Memorial Studies in Religion, Culture, and Social Development

This series is named for Martin Luther King, Jr., because of his superb scholarship and eminence in Religion and Society, and is designed to promote excellence in scholarly research and writing in areas that reflect the interrelatedness of religion and social/cultural/political development both in the American society and in the world. Examination of and elaboration on religion and socio-cultural components such as race relations, economic development, marital and sexual relations, inter-ethnic cooperation, contemporary political problems, women, Black American, Native American, and Third World issues, and the like are welcomed. Manuscripts submitted must be equal in size to a 200 to 425 page book. Two copies must be submitted.

Mozella G. Mitchell
Religious Studies Department 310 CPR
University of South Florida
Tampa, Florida 33620